HITLER'S WAR MACHINE

PANZERS AT WAR
1939-1942

BY BOB CARRUTHERS

Pen & Sword
MILITARY

This edition published in 2013 by
Pen & Sword Military
An imprint of
Pen & Sword Books Ltd
47 Church Street
Barnsley
South Yorkshire
S70 2AS

First published in Great Britain in 2011 in digital format by
Coda Books Ltd.

ISBN 978 1 78159 130 7

Printed and bound by CPI Group (UK) Ltd, Croydon, CR0 4YY

Pen & Sword Books Ltd incorporates the Imprints of Pen & Sword Aviation, Pen &
Sword Family History, Pen & Sword Maritime, Pen & Sword Military, Pen & Sword
Discovery, Pen & Sword Politics, Pen & Sword Atlas, Pen & Sword Archaeology,
Wharncliffe Local History, Wharncliffe True Crime, Wharncliffe Transport, Pen & Sword
Select, Pen & Sword Military Classics, Leo Cooper, The Praetorian Press, Claymore Press,
Remember When, Seaforth Publishing and Frontline Publishing

For a complete list of Pen & Sword titles please contact
PEN & SWORD BOOKS LIMITED
47 Church Street, Barnsley, South Yorkshire, S70 2AS, England
E-mail: enquiries@pen-and-sword.co.uk
Website: www.pen-and-sword.co.uk

CONTENTS

INTRODUCTION

A NEW THREAT

In April 1938, to mark the Führer's birthday, Hitler's magnificent new army marched before him. At the centre of the great parade were the tanks of the new German Panzer Divisions. The event was staged to intimidate the world. True, most of the tanks were small and lightly armed and, unbeknownst to the foreign dignitaries, some were allegedly driven past twice, but they served Hitler's grand design. Hitler was a gambler and he gambled upon bluffing his enemies into believing his tank forces were far stronger than they actually were. By a combination of deceit and brinkmanship. Hitler had made a chilling and spectacular assertion of Germany's re-born military might.

Adolf Hitler was the man who provided the impetus to develop the Panzer Divisions of Germany's Wehrmacht, and in the campaigns of the early war years these new tank armies would strike down all before them. The German soldier would become accustomed to fighting against numerical odds but he would also become accustomed to victory. The comparatively few mechanised and armoured units were the only truly modem component of the German Army and they were the key to much of its extraordinary success. The military of many countries were familiar with wireless, with tanks and with war planes, but only in Germany were these elements so effectively combined to form fully integrated fighting units with exceptional striking power. Hitler's Generals had rewritten the rule book of battle. In Poland it took less than a month to dispose of a large but poorly equipped Polish army which had fought along rigidly traditional lines. In France, the German army successfully challenged the largest and most modern army in Europe. In the ensuing 'Blitzkrieg' or 'lightning war' the British forces were completely routed. Only a year later even this achievement was to be eclipsed by Germany's astonishing victories in the war against Stalin's Soviet Union. In June 1941, spearheaded by tank formations, German Armies swept eastward. In a series of huge encirclements, thousands of Soviet tanks were destroyed and millions of Soviet troops killed or captured. For a while it seemed that Hitler would succeed where Napoleon had failed, by conquering the vast eastern power. On the world stage the tank had become established as a symbol of German invincibility.

Panzer III chassis in the Alkett works during 1941.

It is difficult now to imagine that such small and lightly armoured tanks could spearhead the devastating operation of Blitzkrieg. The secret of their success was speed and co-ordination of effort. In reality, the remarkable string of German successes was due less to superiority of military technology than to the excellence of German methods and training. Many of the German Panzer Division were equipped only with Panzer 1 and II light tanks. It was the new way of waging war which came as a hammer blow to Germany's opponents, forcing them to radically rethink their own military tactics. Slowly the lessons would be learned and eventually the answer to Blitzkrieg would be found.

Tanks came of age in the Second World War. They also developed quicker and changed more in a six-year period than at any time before or since. The catalyst was the demands of a

Tanks of the Panzerwaffe silhouetted against the skyline during the advance to Stalingrad in August 1942.

technological war. Like a crazed version of Darwin's Theory of Evolution, the Second World War accelerated the pace of design. Fast responses to a constantly changing situation were urgently needed and new designs had to be engineered, tested and built in an incredibly short timescale. In the space of three short years, German tank technology progressed from the lightweight and inefficient Panzer I to the mighty Panzer VI - the Tiger, the most complete fighting vehicle of the war. As an example of evolution, the transformation of the Panzer 1 to the Tiger was an almost unbelievable leap in design terms.

DARWINISM GONE MAD

At the end of the nineteenth century when he proposed his theory of evolution, Charles Darwin noted that there were many branches that led to unsuccessful species and hence to extinction. Of course, Darwin was talking about animals, but tanks, it would seem, followed broadly the same rules of evolution.

In the 20's and 30's, it was understood that tanks in the coming war would need to be able to deal with two major situations. The first were tank-versus-tank actions. Even the lightest tanks were capable of surviving explosions very close to the vehicle. Faced with the armour of a tank, explosive shell power alone was therefore of little value. To destroy a tank, it was obviously necessary to fire a projectile fast enough to penetrate the armour of the hull and disable the machine, or kill the men inside. Elementary physics tells us that force equals mass times velocity. For the job of destroying other tanks, the tank needs to be able to fire the heaviest practicable shell, at huge speeds. This produces enough force to punch through the armour of an enemy tank. Explosive power alone has little value against the thick armour of a tank. What gives the missile its penetrating power is the enormous velocity which slices through the armour of enemy vehicles. Even today, armour piercing rounds still tend to be solid shot which rely upon a very high velocity, and the enormous pressures and heat created by a round impacting on armour, in order to burn its way or melt its way through the armour to fly around inside, either destroying equipment or killing or injuring the crew.

The armour of most tanks of 1939 and 1940 vintage could be penetrated by relatively small calibre anti-tank weapons, but the armour piercing weapons which fire these high velocity shells were only useful in combat against other tanks. A variety of high explosive anti-tank rounds were therefore developed, which were designed to first penetrate the armour of an enemy tank, then explode inside the vehicle. This fine balancing act was rarely achieved in practice, and it is debatable whether the small amount of explosive contained in the shells was much more effective than the massive kinetic impact of a high velocity round.

In addition to other tanks, tanks needed to be able to deal with infantry and field guns. In these cases they needed to be able to fire a high explosive round. Here, the speed of the shell was less important; what mattered was the weight of explosive packed into the warhead. In simple terms, the bigger the shell, the bigger the explosion. High explosive shells - generally speaking - had a hollow cone into which high explosives were inserted and which were designed to detonate and throw out a lethal stream of metal splinters, which were particularly effective against infantry out in the open. Of course, high explosives were also useful for destroying non-armoured targets such as lorries and jeeps.

The drive to achieve the combination of destructive power and a tank-killing capability produced two radically different alternatives. Some countries opted for a balanced tank force with some tanks developed for anti-tank duties and others for high explosive capability.

This was certainly the case with the Wehrmacht: the Germans developed two separate types of tank, each specialised for a particular job. The first were the tank killers equipped with a high velocity anti-tank gun with a longer barrel of smaller calibre.

Most of the Panzer IIIs of 1939 vintage were equipped with the 37mm gun, designed to deal with enemy tanks. By contrast all of the heavier Panzer IV tanks were designed as infantry support tanks. They were equipped with a short barrelled 75mm gun, of lower velocity but higher calibre, ideal for firing high explosives.

As the short-barrelled 75mm gun was designed to fire high explosive in the close support role, the Panzer IV had to be made with heavier armour as this tank was designed to stay close to the infantry, and use the gun to deal with the usual infantry opposition, in the form of machine gun positions, block houses and light artillery. Although it did have an anti-tank capability, the early

Kliest's Panzers advance along a railway line during the early stages of Operation Barbarossa. Operating in conjunction with Guderian's forces, these tanks helped to produce some of the largest hauls of prisoners on the Eastern Front.

A group of tank men take a well-earned rest from the pressures of life on the move. The strain of constant action can be seen etched into their faces.

war 75mm gun was not really to be judged as an anti-tank weapon. The Panzer IV was designed to deal with those targets that a high velocity anti-tank gun could not cope with.

In contrast to the Germans, who developed two different types of tanks to do different jobs, one solution tried by the armies of Britain, France, America and Russia was to house two types of gun in the same tank. This produced the massive multi-turreted tanks like the French Char 2c, the Russian BT-35 and the American Lee-Grant tank.

The dual turret idea was a failure, an evolutionary blind alley which was cruelly exposed on the battlefield. The two turrets made the tank difficult to operate, it was impossible to co-ordinate the guns and the sheer size of the machines presented a huge target that was difficult to miss. With the figure of her commander perched some 15 feet above the ground, it was easy to see why the Lee-Grant tank could not be successfully hidden on the battlefield.

As the war progressed, the same course was ultimately adopted by all sides, which was to combine both an anti-tank capability and an infantry support role in one well armoured vehicle which mounted the largest possible calibre of main gun with the highest practicable velocity. The larger calibre effectively gave it a good high explosive firing capability and the high velocity gave it a deadly killing power against other tanks. The Panther tank of 1944 vintage was considered by many to be the ultimate combination of these two features.

Despite the undoubted promise of machines like the Panther, in 1945, when the war ended, Germany was still developing the super heavy Panzer VII, a huge metal monster, weighing over one hundred tons, massively armoured and sporting a huge 122mm main gun. In an untypically humorous moment, this machine, designed to lead the Nazi war machine, was nicknamed 'Maus' (Mouse). The Maus was never to see action and only four prototypes were built, but it seemed that the crazed minds of the Third Reich would never give up the quest to be the best and the biggest, whatever the cost, but as the humble T-34 had proved, in matters of evolution, sometimes quantity matters as much as quality.

TANK TERMINOLOGY

Some common phrases and terms with their English counterparts might prove helpful:

- **Abteilung (Abt)**
Detachment / Battalion

- **Ausfuhrung (Ausf)**
Variant of Model

- **Begleitwagen**
Codename for Panzer I

- **Beobachtungswagen (Beob.Wg)**
Observation Post Vehicle

- **Bergepanzer**
Armoured Recovery Vehicle

- **Beutepanzer**
Captured tanks

- **Fliegerabwehrkanone (Flak)**
Anti-Aircratft Gun

- **Geschutzwagen (Gw.)**
Gun vehicle

- **Granatwerfer (Gr.W)**
Mortar / Rocket Projector

- **Jagdpanzer(Jgd. Pz)**
Tank destroyer

- **(Mun Pz.)**
Ammunition Carrier

- **Osketten**
58mm wide tracks for use in Russia
(Spring of 1944)

- **Panzerabwehrkanone (Pak)**
Anti-Tank Gun

- **Panzer-Befehlswagen (Pz.BefWg)**
Command Tank

- **Panzerjäger (Pz.Jag)**
Tank Hunter

- **Panzcrjagdkanone (Pjk)**
Anti- tank Gun (itself)

- **Panzerkampfwagen (PzKpfw)**
Battle Tank

- **Panzersphwagen (PSW)**
Armoured Car

- **Personenkraftwagen (Pzw)**
Personel Carrier

- **Schurzen**
Skirts / Aprons

- **Schutzenpanzerwagen**
Half-Tracked Personnel Carrier

- **Schutzenzug (zug)**
Platoon

- **schwere (s)**
Heavy

- **Selbstfahrlafette (sf)**
Self Propelled Gun

- **Sonderkraftfahrzeng (SdKfz)**
Special Purpose Motor Vehicle

- **Sturmgeschütz (StuG)**
Assault Gun

- **Sturm-Infanteriegeschutz (SIG)**
Assault Infantry Gun

- **Sturmpanzerhaubitze (StuK)**
Assault Howitzer

- **Sturmpanzerkanone (StuK)**
Assault Gun (itself)

- **Tauchpanzer**
A submersible tank

- **Waffantrager**
Weapon Carrier

- **Werkstatt-Kompanie**
Maintenance Company

- **Winterketten**
560mm wide tracks for use in Russia
(Fall of 1942)

- **Versuchskonstruktion (VK)**
Experimental Construction / Prototype

- **Vollkettenfahrzeug (VK)**
Full-Tracked Vehicle

THE PANZER DIVISIONS

"In general, the tanks have proven their worth. The capabilities and overall manoeuvrability of the vehicles is very good. The MG-Kampfwagens are very useful and effective vehicles. However, it should not be overlooked that armour defeating weapons and weapons firing high explosives must be introduced."

GENERAL LUTZ, KOMMANDO DER PANZERTRAPPEN, AUGUST 1935

In the wake of the bitter defeat inflicted on Germany in the Great War the allied forces were determined that there should be no repeat of that terrible conflict. The treaty of Versailles imposed draconian limitations on the Germans, strictly limiting the overall size of the army, and, more importantly, limiting the types of weaponry to be allowed. The events of the Great War had clearly identified the powerful effect of the advent of air power; the result was that Germany was to be denied access to an air force. Despite the fact that the war had seen no major tank-versus-tank battles, the Allies had seen enough to recognise the potential of the tank as a device capable of achieving major strategic impact in future wars. As a consequence, these new weapons were added to the growing list of items denied to the German forces.

Even in the 20's it was already apparent that, for a modern army, the consequences of entering into battle without tanks could be disastrous. This, of course, was the object of the Versailles Treaty, which only permitted Germany a small standing army for the purpose of internal peacekeeping and national defence. However, as the High Command understood all too well, without a tank force the chances of a successful counter attack were slim and for a nation born to the notion of aggressive moves even on the strategic defensive, this was really one step too far. It was this concern which initially shaped the drive for a German tank force. Later these foundations would

The forerunners of the mighty Panzer Divisions. Forbidden to develop an armoured force, the Wehrmacht had to resort to the humiliating solution of wood and cardboard frames placed over the chassis of conventional automobiles. The first training exercises took place using these bizarre vehicles.

be usurped by Hitler for his own purposes. Obviously the leaders of the Wehrmacht could not accept the humiliating conditions of the Versailles treaty without demur, and there began a period of covert experimentation which was to lead to the development of a tank capability that would shake the world.

SOVIET CO-OPERATION

Ironically, the roots of the German Panzerwaffe were laid in conjunction with Soviet Russia, the nation that was destined to become Nazi Germany's greatest enemy and ultimately her nemesis. During the 20's the new Soviet Union was an even greater pariah than Germany, and the fledgling soviet state had already withstood the perils of a civil war and foreign intervention, which had seen British ground troops deployed in an attempt to assist the White Russians. Clearly Moscow could not look to London or Paris for aid, so she turned instead to her former adversary, and German/Soviet tank development began at Kazan, located deep inside Russia where secrecy was relatively easy to maintain.

In April 1926 the first technical specifications had been given for what was eventually to become the Panzer IV. It was given the code name Armeewagen 20 and in March 1927 the first contracts for the design of two experimental machines each were given to Daimler Benz, Krupp and Rheinmetall. These machines were given the code name Grosstraktor and each was to have a 7.5cm gun in a fully traversable turret. The first six Grosstraktor were completed in July 1929 and immediately transported to the secret training grounds at Kama, near Kazan. These machines were the predecessors of the Panzer IV, which was to function effectively throughout the war years.

Although tank design had been exposed to a considerable deal of practical action during the Great War, without a clear indication of how tank-to-tank combat might develop there were a number of competing schools of thought. One favoured large multi-turreted tanks which could perform a number of functions on the battlefield. Others favoured specialist machines for reconnaissance, close support and anti-tank duties. Clearly the Grosstraktor could not fulfil the reconnaissance role. So, in May 1928 the first orders for the design of a lighter tank, code named Leichttraktor were given: this time only Krupp and Rheinmetall were given the order to proceed to complete two prototypes. In May 1930 the two machines were completed and transported secretly to Kazan, where they arrived in June 1930. Very quickly a glaring design fault with the Leichttraktors became apparent. The drive sprocket for the tracks was located at the back of the vehicle, where it was more likely to shed the track. The location of the engine at the front of the tank was also considered to be a particularly dangerous proposition. A new design was therefore specified in September 1931 which became known as the Kleintraktor. This machine had the drive at the front and the engine in the rear, an arrangement which was to become the standard in tank design for the next 60 years. The Kleintraktor was to become the forerunner of the Panzerkampfwagen I, and the first experimental machine was completed by Krupp in September 1932. In the secrecy of the tank-proving grounds at Kama the Germans were able to make a great deal of progress on the technical aspects of tank design. At the same time, of course, the crews and officers were receiving practical training in the use of tanks in battle and, crucially, the cooperation between the machines. It was not until 1928, however, that the Reichswehr secretly began to formulate a five-year plan which would lead to the creation of the first tank companies by 1933.

Eventually the first Panzer training unit was born on 1st November 1933, under conditions of extreme secrecy, and was given the code-name Kraftfahrlehrkommando Zossen. It was comprised mainly of officers and men who had taken part in the Russian experiment. At the time of the unit's formation only a very limited number of machines were available. These comprised four Grosstraktor, four Leichttraktor V and six of the Kleintraktor chassis, which had no turrets. Clearly this was not going to be sufficient to develop a tank force; however, the delivery of the first 150 Kleintraktor chassis for driver training commenced in January 1934, from which point the rapid expansion of the tank forces could proceed apace. The first organisation charts for an experimental armoured division were distributed within the army on 12 October 1934, although most of the units were still known by cover names; officially, the Panzer Division were styled as a Cavalry Division.

At the outset the Panzer division was to be composed of two armoured regiments which were supported by a light motorised infantry regiment, a motorcycle battalion, an anti-tank battalion, a reconnaissance battalion, a light artillery regiment, a signals battalion and a light combat engineer company, and there was even a plan for a self-propelled artillery battalion, which was very radical at this time. Already it was obvious that the Panzer division would require an enormous logistical tail, and the first divisions required a strength of 13,000 officers and men, which needed 4,000 field vehicles and 481 tracked vehicles to be able to function effectively. Clearly the creation and maintenance of a number of Panzer divisions was going to be an enormous undertaking. It was also something which could not be achieved in short timescales as there were limits to the number of tanks which could be manufactured. Unfortunately for Germany. Adolf Hitler was very much a man in a hurry.

DEVELOPMENT OF THE TANK FORCE

The first vehicle to be produced in any numbers was the tiny Panzer I, which at the time was known as the MG Panzerwagen. Delivery of 318 of these had been made by August 1935, along with 15 of the Zugfuhrerwagen, which was later to become the Panzer III. One aspect of tank design which the Germans got absolutely right from the very outset was to identify the importance of radio communications. Although initially only the command tanks were filled with radios that could both transmit and receive, the other vehicles were at last equipped with receiving radio sets, and this was a major advance upon the thinking of many of the countries which would come to oppose Germany. Throughout 1934 exercises continued with the experimental tank units and a number of other valuable lessons quickly became apparent, particularly the need for close co-operation between the air forces and the tanks on the ground. At this point the first serious tank tactics which were to bring so much success during the Second World War began to appear. It was soon obvious that the tanks needed to be employed on a relatively narrow front. A divisional front was estimated at about three kilometres, a great change from the wide fronts of the Great War. It was still obvious to the German High Command that the decisions which were being made, were on theory, rather than practice. Germany - and indeed every other nation of the time - had no

A rare image of one of the six Grosstraktor manufactured by Rhinemettal during 1928 and 1929. All six were used in the secret testing programme at Kama.

The cardboard tanks used to begin the process of training the future Panzerwaffe during the early 1920s. The three parts are about to be locked over the car frame to produce the pathetic vehicles seen on page 9.

practical experience to draw on, therefore a number of educated guesses were made. In January 1936 General Beck reported to the High Command, his findings being based on a study of a French organisation. He was also very critical of the slow rise in production capacity which was hampering the development of the tank force. Interestingly, the debate about which tasks tanks were suitable for, and whether specialist machines had to be developed for each task was already beginning to take shape. Beck's report clearly stated that the three main tasks of the Panzers were supporting infantry, operating in units with other mobile weapons and, finally, combating tanks. Beck himself was unable to come to a decision about whether a single tank should he adapted for each of these purposes or whether a specialist vehicle should he designed for each purpose. Ultimately the decision was that the light tanks would be used in a scouting role and that an infantry support tank would be developed which was ultimately to come in the form of the Panzer IV. This left the Panzer III as the main battle tank. Amazingly the decision was taken that the 3.7cm gun which initially equipped the Panzer III would be sufficient for the battle conditions. The various types of German tank design were to cater for most eventualities on the battlefield. The Panzer I and II were earmarked for the reconnaissance role. The Panzer III was essentially for anti-tank operations and the Panzer IV was designed to provide close support for the infantry. Almost from the outset the limitations of the design for the Panzer I were obvious. The armament in the form of two machine guns, was inadequate for most purposes on the battlefield. In addition the very thin armour gave protection only against rifle bullets: almost any battlefield weapon could penetrate the armour. More significant was the fact that the crew was comprised of only two men.

THE CLOSED WORLD

The world of the tank man is a world of very limited vision. With the hatches open, a tank commander can use the height advantage of his vehicle to scan the terrain for miles around. However, once the tank is threatened and the hatches have to be closed, the view of the world is through tiny vision slits, which makes visual recognition extremely difficult. There are a number

PANZERKAMPFWAGEN SD.KFZ.101

In 1931, Major-General Oswald Lutz was appointed "Inspector of Motor Transport" in the German Army (Reichswehr) with Heinz Guderian as his Chief of Staff. Both realised the need for the creation of the German Armoured Forces and a light training tank in which to train future personnel of Panzer Divisions. In 1932, specifications for a light (5-ton) tank were made and issued to Rheinmetall, Krupp. Henschel. MAN and Daimler Benz. The designers' work was based on experiences from co-operation with Swedish Landsverk Company and previous "secret" projects.

In 1933, the Heereswaffenamt ordered the development of the Kleintraktor - an armoured vehicle between 4 and 7 tons in weight. It was designated as the La.S. (Landwirtschaftlicher Schlepper I La.S. - agricultural tractor) to hide its true purpose from the Treaty of Versailles. Rheinmetall, Krupp, Henschel, MAN and Daimler Benz submitted their prototypes which were all similar in design. It was Krupp's design of the LKA I which was selected.

The design of the LKA I was partially based on the British Carden Loyd Mk. IV tankette chassis two of which were secretly purchased from Russia in 1932. Krupp's design was then once again modified and in the summer of 1933, five La.S. chassis were produced and tested at Kummersdorf. It was then decided to mount Krupp's chassis with the Daimler-Benz's superstructure and turret.

In February 1934 further tests were performed and in April the improved LKA I (La.S.), known as the MG Panzerwagen - Versuchkraftfahrzeug 617 entered production. On entering production it was renamed the Pz.Kpfw I Ausf A. In April 1934, 15 were produced and all were presented to Adolf Hitler by Heinz Guderian.

The Panzer I was produced in two main very similar variants the Ausf A (1934) and the Ausf B (1935), which both had different suspensions and engines. In 1935/36, the Panzer I Ausf A was experimentally mounted with a Krupp M601 diesel engine, it could only produce 45hp of power, and the idea of a diesel powered vehicle was rejected.

The debut for the Pz.Kpfw I in a combat situation took place during the Spanish Civil War, 1936/38, where both the tank and the tactic of Blitzkrieg were put to the test. Approximately 100 Ausf A, Ausf B and Kleiner Panzer Befehlswagen I tanks saw service with the Condor Legion (Major Ritter von Thomas' Panzer Abteilung 88 also known as Abteilung Drohne) and General Franco's Nationalists. They were, however, outclassed by the Soviet T-26 and BT-5 provided to the Republicans. Some Pz.Kpfw Is which were captured by the Republicans were rearmed with French Hotchkiss 25mm guns mounted in a modified turret.

It was also at this time that the Pz.Kpfw I Ausf B was experimentally armed with 20mm Breda gun mounted in a modified turret, in order to increase its combat potential.

The Pz.Kpfw were allocated to two Nationalist tank battalions, the Agrupacion de Carros - 1st and 2nd Tank Battalions.

Following the Spanish Civil War it was obvious that the Panzer 1 did not have any potential as a combat tank and a further programme development into a fast reconnaissance and light infantry tank was started.

This began with the introduction of the Ausf C, Ausf D and Ausf F, completely new designs sharing only a limited number of components with the standard Panzer 1 Ausf B. The Panzer 1 Ausf C - neuer Art (VK 601) was produced by Krauss-Maffei and Daimler-Benz from late 1942 to early 1943 with only 40(46) being produced. The Ausf D - neuer Art verstarkt (VK 602) was an up-armoured and improved version of the Ausf C which was produced in limited numbers. The Panzer 1 Ausf F - neuer Art verstarkt (up-armoured new model) (VK 1801) was produced by Daimler Benz and Krauss-Maffei from April 1942 to January 1943 with only 30 being produced.

In mid 1943, a small number of Ausf C and Ausf F were combat tested with the 1st and 2nd Panzer Division fighting on the Eastern Front and later served in Yugoslavia. A number of Pz.Kpfw I Ausf C ended up in Normandy with LVIII Panzer Corps, where they were lost in 1944. The Ausf C, D and F never entered full production. Today, the Pz.Kpfw I Ausf F can be seen in the Museum of Armoured Forces in Kubinka near Moscow in Russia.

The Panzer I was the main tank of the German army during the Polish Campaign with some 1445 in service (as such they provided approximately 50% of all tanks in service). During the African campaign the PzKpfw Is were equipped with larger filters and an improved ventilation system.

In early 1942. Panzer Is were taken out of service and were handed over to the Police and anti-partisan units; those without superstructures were handed over to para-military organizations such as NSKK (National Socialist Motor Corps) for training purposes. A total of 511 PzKpfw I turrets

CONVERSIONS

In 1939/40, 100 PzKpfw I Ausf A/B were converted into Ladungsleger I (Ladungsleger auf Panzerkampfwagen I Ausf A or B / zerstorerpanzer) - a 50kg explosive charge layer vehicle. They were especially designed for engineer units to provide them with the charge carrier for delayed action explosives and saw combat service during the Blitzkrieg in the West with 7th Panzer Division and then in Russia.

During the African campaign, at the Battle of Tobruk, a small number of Panzerkampfwagen I Ausf As were converted in the field by the Africa Korps 5th Light Division into Flammenwerfer auf Panzerkampfwagen I Ausf A. It was armed with light portable infantry Flammenwerfer (flamethrower model) 40 and an MG, in place of right hand machine gun. Some 10 to 12 bursts could be fired with a range of 25 metres.

The most radical conversion based on the modified PzKpfw I Ausf A was the Flakpanzer I (Sd. Kfz. 101) armed with a 20mm Flak 38 L/1 12.5 sun. It was based on the modified Munitionsschlepper 1 Ausf A (Sd.Kfz.l 11) a light ammunition carrier. Approximately 24 were produced in early 1941 by Alkett in Berlin and all went into equipping three

Panzer I Ausf A. in combat during the German invasion of Norway

batteries of the 614th Flak Abteilung with eight vehicles each. The last of those interesting conversions was lost at Stalingrad in January of 1943. A PzKpfw I was also modified and mounted with a 15mm MG 151115 Drilling heavy machine gun. It was captured on the Eastern Front in 1943.

Armour (mm/angle) Ausf A.
Front Turret: 13/10
Front Upper Hull: 13/22
Front Lower Hull: 13/27
Side Turret: 13/22
Side Upper Hull: 13/22
Side Lower Hull: 13/0
Rear Turret: 13/22
Rear Upper Hull: 13/17
Rear Lower Hull: 13/15
Turret Top/ Bottom: 8/82
Upper Hull Top / Bottom: 6/82
Lower Hull Top / Bottom: 6/90
Gun Mantlet: 13/round

Armour (mm/angle) Ausf B.
Front Turret: 13/10
Front Upper Hull: 13/22
Front Lower Hull: 13/27
Side Turret: 13/22
Side Upper Hull: 13/22
Side Lower Hull: 13/0
Rear Turret: 13/22
Rear Upper Hull: 13/0
Rear Lower Hull: 13/19
Turret Top / Bottom: 8/82
Upper Hull Top / Bottom: 6/83
Lower Hull Tip / Bottom: 6/90
Gun Mantlet: 13/round

Model	Panzer I Ausf A.	Panzer I Ausf B.
Weight	5300 kg	5900 kg
Crew	2	2
Engine	Krupp M305 (Boxer) 4-cylinder / 57 hp	Maybach NL38TR 6-cylinder / 100hp
Speed	37 km/h	40km/h
Range	Road: 200 km Crosscountry: 140 km	Road: 180 km Crosscountry: 130 km
Fuel	144 litres	146 litres
Capacity	3, 460 cc	3, 790 cc
Length	4.02 m	4.43 m
Width	2.06 m	2.06 m
Height	1.72 m	1.72 m
Armament	(7.92 mm)	(7.92mm)
Ammunition Supply	2250 rounds (MG)	2250 rounds (MG)

Model	Production Period	No. of chassis produced	No. of Pz.Kpfw. I produced
Ausf A	1934 - 1936	1477	818
Ausf B	1935 - 1939	6023	675
Ausf C (VK 601)	1942 - 1943	40	40
Ausf D (VK 602)	1942 - 1943	Prototype stage	-
Ausf F (VK 1801)	1942 - 1943	30	30

Variants of Panzerkampfwagen I (Sd. Kfz. 101)	
Ausf A (July 1934 - June 1936)	• 2x MG13 Dreyse (7.92mm) • 57hp Krupp M305 (Boxer) Engine • 4 road wheels & 3 return rollers
Ausf B (August 1935 - June 1937)	• 2x MG13 Dreyse (7.92mm) • 100hp Maybach NL 38 TR Engine • 5 road wheels & 4 return rollers • Lengthened and redesigned hull
Ausf A/B (1935 - 1937) Befehlswagen / Command Tank	• 1x MG13 Dreyse or MG34 (7.92mm) • 57hp Krupp M305 (Boxer) Engine - Ausf A • 100hp Maybach NL 38 TR Engine - Ausf B • 4 road wheels & 3 return rollers - Ausf A • 5 road wheels & 4 return rollers - Ausf B
Ausf C (nA) (July 1942 - December 1942)	• 2x MG13 Dreyse (7.92mm) • 57hp Krupp M305 (Boxer) Engine • 4 road wheels & 3 return rollers
Ausf D (nA verst) (1942 - 1943)	• 2x MG13 Dreyse (7.92mm) • 57hp Krupp M305 (Boxer) Engine • 4 road wheels & 3 return rollers
Ausf F (nA verst) (April 1942 - January 1943)	• 2x MG13 Dreyse (7.92mm) • 57hp Krupp M305 (Boxer) Engine • 4 road wheels & 3 return rollers

Panzer I's seen here during the march past Adolf Hitler in front of a jubilant crowd in Vienna, March 1938.

CONVERSIONS

- **Munitionsschlepper I Ausf A (Sd.Kfz 111)** - light ammunition carrier
- **Kleine Panzer Befahlswagen I (Sd.Kfz. 265)** - light command tank
- **Sanitatskraftwagen I (Sd.Kfz. 265)** - armoured ambulance
- **Pionier-Kampfwagen I** - engineer tank
- **Panzerjäger I (Sd.Kfz. 101)** - 47mm Pak gun carrier
- **Panzerjäger I** - 37mm Pak gun carrier
- **Sturmpanzer I Bison (Sd.Kfz. 101)** - 150mm sIG 33 gun carrier
- **Leichte Bergepanzer I** - light recovery vehicle
- **Instandsetzungstrupp I** - troop carrier / recovery vehicle
- **Fahreschulewagen I** - training tank
- **Jadungsleger auf PzKpfw I Ausf A/B (zerstorerpanzer)** - explosive charge layer
- **Minenraumer I Ausf B** - mine clearing vehicle (50 produced in 1938)
- **Brueckenleger I auf PzKpfw 1 Ausf A** - light bridging vehicle (2 produced in 1939)
- **Flakpanzer 1 Ausf A (Sd.Kfz 101)** - 20mm Flak 38 anti-aircraft tank
- **Flammeemwerfer auf PzKpfw I Ausf A** - flamethrower tank

Panzer I Ausf B.

Inside the German tank works in 1939. In the background are large numbers of Panzer IIIs under construction. The machine in the foreground is an experimental Nebau Panzerkampfwagen, not destined for active service. Its prominence is probably not accidental and may have been designed to confuse enemy intelligence services.

of tasks which need to be carried out in the tank. Communication, both inwards and outwards, with other vehicles in the formation is absolutely essential and, with the rudimentary radio equipment of the period, this was really a full-time job. In addition to operating the radio, the commander had to be surveying the ground ahead for the driver, and in addition he was expected to operate the machine guns. In simple terms, this was far too many tasks for one man to hope to successfully master during the heat of an engagement. The Panzer 1 had already shown its limitations, and in fairness it was never really intended as a frontline battle tank. Its purpose, really, was as a training tank, and the numbers ordered were in response to the need to train a large number of men quickly. It was only Hitler's ambitious brinkmanship that would propel the Army into having to press the Panzer I into a service for which it was plainly inadequate; even in 1936 this was obvious for all to see.

The successor to the Panzer I in the reconnaissance role should of course have been the Panzer II. The Panzer II was therefore a slight advance on this sorry state of affairs in that it was a three-man machine which allowed for a driver as well as a gunner and the commander. Although this was some improvement it was still not a great advance on the Panzer I. The 20mm cannon could at least penetrate light tanks, but it really lacked the hitting power for serious tank-to-tank engagements. Above all, here were still too few men in the vehicle to conduct all of the tasks satisfactorily. Really, a four-man crew was the absolute minimum and events would quickly demonstrate that five was the number that should be deployed in a modem tank. As early as October 1935 General Liese, head of the Heeres Waffenamt issued a report which gave the limitations of the tanks. He noted that the MG Panzerwagen (Panzer I), although fitted out only with two 7.9mm machine guns, could be adapted to attack armoured cars and other light tanks if it was issued with special S.M.P. steel core ammunition. In the case of the MG Panzer II, it was noted that the muzzle velocity of the 2cm gun could penetrate up to 10mm of armoured plate at a range of up to 700 metres. It was therefore decided that the Panzer II could engage armoured ears with success, and was also fully functional for combat against tanks with approximately the same armour as itself. Liese noted that the tanks most likely to be encountered in large numbers in a war against the French were the light Renault Ml7 and Ml8 tanks, of which there were about three thousand operational in the French forces at the time. It was also thought that the Panzer 11 would be the equal of the Renault NC37 and NC31 tanks. Against the heavier French tanks, including the Char B, it was noted that the Panzer II was practically worthless. Despite these reservations large-scale delivery of the Panzer II was already in train and was expected to commence from 1st April 1937. As regards the new Panzer III, which was designed to be the main battle tank, it was obvious that Liese was already beginning to have reservations about the effectiveness of the 37mm gun. Originally the 37mm L/45 had been planned for this vehicle but it was urged that the experimental tanks be upgraded to include the L/65 version, which gave a much higher muzzle velocity and some real prospect of penetrating the 40mm thick armoured plate of the new French medium tanks. With this in mind it was obvious at this stage that a 50mm gun would be a better proposition for the Panzer III; however the addition of the larger gun would demand a significant increase in the diameter of the turret which would in turn mean radical redevelopment of the chassis. Given the pressures of time and the need to equip the formations quickly Liese came to the conclusion that the 37mm L/65 was the favoured route, although it is interesting that the limitations of its design had already been noted.

Despite the difficult conditions, the fledgling German tank Forces had managed to develop

Panzer Is roll through the Uber den Ring, Vienna, March 1938.

some innovations of their own. Influential sections of the officer corps could see the advantages that the tank could bring to the next war and they developed new theories that centred on the use of the tank, theories that would revolutionise the way wars would be fought. Despite the problems of convincing his superiors of the advantages of the tank, Heinz Guderian in particular stuck to his secretive task. With determined persistence, and the help of some impressive demonstration exercises, he finally convinced both the German General Staff and Adolf Hitler that the tank could help to win future wars.

When Hitler precipitated the Second World War with his invasion of Poland in 1939, his tank forces were questionable at best, but the gamble succeeded by the application of a new tactical doctrine - championed by General Heinz Guderian - which was to become known as Blitzkrieg.

Blitzkrieg also evolved at least partially from a re-assessment of war tactics that took place not only in Germany, but in Russia and Britain as well. Two perceptive British military theorists. Major General J.C. Fuller and Captain B. Liddell Hart, understood that the introduction of the tank during the First World War had opened up hitherto undreamed of military possibilities.

As a result of Guderian's efforts, in 1935 the first Panzer Divisions were formed. These revolutionary formations incorporated a Tank Brigade with 561 tanks to provide the main firepower. A great deal of accurate thought had gone into the development of the Panzer Division, which also included motorised infantry, reconnaissance and artillery. The resulting Panzer Division was a well-balanced force which could call on the support of any or all of the component parts to capture an objective. The purpose of the Panzer Division was to launch a speedy advance, break through into enemy territory and spread confusion, fear and panic in the enemy command and communication systems. One further innovation was the close link with the Luftwaffe, who could add even more firepower when needed.

THE PANZER DIVISONS ARE FORMED

On 15 October 1935 the first three Panzer Divisions were formed. General-Colonel Maximilian Von Weichs commanded the 1st Panzer Division with its headquarters in Weimar, the 2nd Panzer Division was commanded by Colonel Heinz Guderian and had its headquarters in Wurzburg. General-Colonel Ernst Fessmann commanded the 3rd Panzer Division, with his headquarters in Berlin.

The tank component of the first Panzer divisions was to be a Panzer Brigade, initially composed of two tank regiments. The regiments were, in turn, sub-divided into two Abteilungs (battalions); each Abteilung had four companies with 32 light tanks. The entire brigade strength was 561 tanks including command tanks.

The tank element of the 1st Panzer Division was the 1st Panzer Brigade, which was composed of the 1st Panzer Regiment, stationed in Erfurt, and the 2nd Panzer Regiment, stationed in Eisenach.

The 2nd Panzer Division incorporated the 2nd Panzer Brigade, which was composed of the 3rd Panzer Regiment in Kamenz and the 4th Panzer Regiment stationed in Ohrdruf.

The tank strength of the 3rd Panzer Division, also known as Panzer Brigade 'Berlin', was composed of the 5th Panzer Regiment 'Wundsdorf', stationed in Wunsdorf and the 6th Panzer Regiment (later known as 'Neuruppin') stationed in Zossen.

In 1936 there was a re-shuffle of bases. The 3rd Panzer Regiment was moved to Bamberg, the 4th Panzer Regiment to Schweinfurt and the 6th Panzer Regiment to Neuruppin.

In February and March of 1936 all of the new Panzer units took in extensive training exercises on the proving grounds at Staumuhlcn.

Almost from the outset, and while they were still forming and training, the Panzer units had to be prepared for operational service. The first of these emergencies appeared on 7 March 1936, when German infantry units marched into the demilitarised Rhineland. The Panzer regiments were held on alert in the Senna district but were stood down after four weeks. For the remainder of 1936 the units were exposed to a programme of intensive training. Of course, the expansion of the Panzer force was limited by the rate of expansion in the number of available tanks. However, although the process of design and development continued, as many as 3000 light tanks had already been produced by the end of 1936 and the construction of the designs of the Panzer III and IV were well under way when the first baptism of fire arose for the fledgling tank force.

THE SPANISH CIVIL WAR

In 1936 the Spanish Civil War flared into life and the leadership of the Nationalist forces asked the governments of both Italy and Germany for military support. Although Germany itself could not afford to take a formal part in the war, units of volunteers were made available in support of the Nationalists. Among them was a Panzer unit, given the code-name Abteilung Drohne, which was officially named Panzer Abteilung 88. It was commanded by Major Ritter von Thoma and it was drawn from the ranks of the 4th and 6th Panzer regiments. Although the men really were volunteers there was no shortage, and there were sufficient men to form a company and a workshop column. The volunteers were transferred on German passenger ships as civilian members of the trade union travel organisation, which worked under the slogan 'Strength Through Joy'. They took with them Panzer I tanks and were disembarked at Seville. The training role was a real one, and the German troops were responsible for training Spanish National troops equipped with captured T-26 Russian tanks. The volunteers themselves first saw action in October 1936 when a few Panzer I tanks were deployed to support the Nationalists in their drive on Madrid. In early 1937 the unit was reinforced to form three combat companies and a support column. The German tanks were used in numbers for the first time on 11 May 1937 when they took part in a concerted attack on the Spanish Communist positions near Eremita. The volunteers remained in Spain for over two years and were returned to Germany only in February 1939. In his first report of the action in Spain sent back to Germany in December 1936 von Thoma was quick to point out the limitations of the Panzer I. He noted that from the very outset a gun armed tank was far superior to the machine gun armed Panzer I, although the disadvantage could be overcome to an extent by issuing specially hardened ammunition which could cleanly penetrate Russian tanks at ranges of about 120-150 metres.

A group of seven Panzer Is serving with Gruppe Thoma in the Spanish campaign during 1937. The many limitations of the Panzer I were clearly demonstrated in the Spanish Civil War, but the lack of a viable alternative meant these machines would see considerable service during the early years of the war.

The high command of the Wehrmacht join Hitler for the march past the new tank formations in Vienna. Right from the Führer; Generaloberst Keitel, Reichsführer der SS Himmler, Generaloberst von Brauchitsch, Generaloberst Milch, General Kraub and Reichsstatthalter Dr. Seyss-Inquart.

The Russian tanks, however, quickly adapted their tactics and were able to stay out of range, moving to over a thousand metres away where their superior guns made the Panzer 1 easy prey. The German tanks were particularly vulnerable if the Panzers remained stationary, and von Thoma's orders were to fight constantly on the move. Despite these precautions at least seven Panzers were knocked out by the Russian forces in a single engagement.

The solution to the limitations of the Panzer I in Spain was to attach anti-tank guns to each of the Panzer companies. Once again, with the result of practical experience in the field, von Thoma came to the conclusion that the Panzer I, if it was to be used at all, needed to be accompanied by an infantry support tank which had at least a 7.5cm gun with a range of up to three thousand metres. It was also felt that a better anti-tank gun was needed, with a range of at least 1,500 and not the 900 metres; once again the 37mm gun which was deemed to be inadequate for the task.

Of course the Germans were not the only foreign nationals present in Spain. Both Britain and France had their observers to view the progress of the war. General Fuller wrote an article in the Times on 8 April 1937 which was highly critical of the tanks that were seen in action, particularly the German machines, which Fuller described as 'mobile coffins'. The French went even further and in April 1937 a French newspaper article was particularly critical of the German tanks. It noted that they were a major disappointment because of their slow speed across country and the armour, which was accurately described as almost useless. There was little real defence against enemy anti-tank guns; from a close range even rifle bullets could penetrate them. The French report concluded that although the French tanks were slower they were much better protected and remained 'king of the battle ground'. Altogether approximately one hundred and fifty one Panzer Is were sent to Spain and all were left behind at the close of hostilities.

In the official Report of the Spanish Civil War which was written in March 1939, it was noted that the light tanks were useful only with flamethrowers since it was impossible to fire the machines guns on the move. Once again it was forcefully noted that the Panzer I was an inferior tank. However, during the time of the Spanish Civil War the expansion of the Panzer forces back in Germany continued relatively smoothly, as did the production of the vehicles.

The harsh evidence from the battlefields of Spain did not go unheeded.

As soon as the Panzer II became available from October 1936, resources were immediately switched and there was no effective increase in Panzer I strength, which remained about 1,400 machines until the outbreak of the war. The number of Panzer IIs rose rapidly from 115 in May

1937 to 1,200 in September 1939. Additionally the first of the Panzer IIIs came on stream in October 1937 to be followed by the Panzer IV in January 1938. By the outbreak of the Second World War in September 1939 there were 98 Panzer III in service and 211 Panzer IV, the most useful machines therefore still counting for a tiny proportion of the forces available.

BATTLEFIELD TACTICS

In addition to the increase in the numbers of tanks actually available, the practical application of this new force on the battlefield was also being developed. A report on 24 November 1938 gave the guidelines for the planned use of the Panzer Divisions which were to accomplish a number of primary tasks.

1. They were to be used at the most strategically important sectors and employed in mobile operations.

2. They were to widen and exploit breakthroughs created by infantry reserves.

By now the Army High Command envisaged that nine Panzer Divisions should be available by the Autumn of 1939. The report also made it clear that the Panzertruppen should consist of men that had the highest fighting spirit and that they were to be considered and developed as an elite unit, particularly with regard to their offensive spirit.

Back in Germany, during the autumn of 1936, two new Panzer regiments were formed, 7th Panzer Regiment in Veihingen and 8th Panzer Regiment in Boblingen. The 7th Panzer Regiment was temporarily attached to 1st Panzer Division and the 8th to the 3rd Panzer Division.

From September 14th to 29th 1937, large-scale manoeuvres of the Panzer units took place around Neusterlitz. These were the "Mussolini manoeuvres", named after the Italian dictator who was present. The units involved were the complete 3rd Panzer Division and the 1st Panzer Brigade, from the 1st Panzer Division, who together fielded some 800 Panzer I tanks. On 12 October 1937 a number of new units were formed including the 10th, 11th, 15th and 25th Panzer Regiments, and Panzer Abteilung 65 along with the Panzer Lehr Abteilung. These divisions were earmarked to equip another potentially innovative formation, the Light Division. The habits of the old Cavalry Command died hard and the Light Division was designed to carry out a similar role to the old Cavalry Division in scouting - protecting the flanks of the advance. As such it was equipped with only one tank Abteilung comprising 96 tanks, rather than the two-regiment brigade of a full Panzer Division of 561 tanks.

On 12 March 1938 the Anschluss took Austria into the Reich. The only Panzer unit to take part was 2nd Panzer Division under the command of General Guderian. In preparation for the operation. SS Regiment Leibstandarte Adolf Hitler, commanded by Sepp Dietrich, was attached to the 2nd Panzer Division. The division covered some seven hundred kilometres in 48 hours, but rather ominously lost a third of its tanks due to breakdowns. Fortunately the 2nd Panzer Division was not involved in any combat. Following the Anschluss, Panzer Abteilung 33 was formed from the sole Austrian Panzer Battalion and other members transferred from German units. This unit was stationed in St. Polten. Panzer Abteilung 33 was assigned to the 4th Light Division and later to the 9th Panzer Division formed in Vienna in January 1940. As a result of the expansion of the Reich, the headquarters of the 2nd Panzer Division were now moved to Vienna, and the 3rd and 4th Panzer Regiments were stationed near the cities of Modling and Korneuburg.

The Pz.Kpfw (38)t had been designed and tested before the seizure of Czechoslovakia in 1939. The influx of these valuable machines provided the vital extra numbers which made the early campaigns possible. The 7th and 8th Panzer Divisions used the Pz.Kpfw (38)t in place of the Panzer III during the fall of France.

THE AUSTRIAN PRIZE

Throughout the war the German tank forces were to make considerable use of captured enemy material. Although Austrian armoured fighting vehicles cannot be really labelled as captured since they never took part in any combat and were simply handed over to the Germans, their use represented the beginning of a regular pattern. The first pieces of equipment which fell into German hands were the few Austrian fighting vehicles then in service with Bundesheer. Along with 47 armoured cars there were 74 imported Italian Carro Veloce (CV) 33/35 tankettes designated in Austrian service as Kleinkampfwagen M. 1933 / 1935. These were used to temporarily equip the new Panzer regiments during formation and training. Eventually they were used as ammunition carriers, later some were sold to Hungary.

On 3-4 October 1938 Germany took over the Sudetenland as provided for by the Munich agreement of September 1938. By 10 October the takeover was completed; the only Panzer unit involved this time was the 1st Panzer Division. Once again Hitler breathed a sigh of relief that no armed conflict took place.

In November 1938 Heinz Guderian was promoted to General der Panzertruppen and received his most important assignment, which well may have changed history - he became Chef der Schnellen Truppen (Chief of the Fast Troops). It meant that Guderian was responsible for the recruiting, training and tactics of all the Wehrmacht's motorised and armoured units.

Under his guidance, six new Panzer units were formed. These new units included two new Panzer divisions; the 4th Panzer Division (also known as the 7th Panzer Brigade) was formed on 10th October 1938 at Wurzburg and the 5th Panzer Division (also known as the 8th Panzer Brigade) formed on 25th October 1938 at Oppeln. Also formed were the 4th Panzer Brigade at Stuttgart, the 5th Panzer Brigade at Bamberg, the 6th Panzer Brigade at Wurzburg and the 8th Panzer Brigade at Sagan. In addition, the 23rd. 31st, 35th and 36th Panzer Regiments were also formed along with Panzer Abteilungs 65, 66 and 67.

The 4th Panzer Division incorporated the 7th Panzer Brigade, composed of the 35th and 36th Panzer Regiments commanded by General Major George Hans Reinhardt. The new 5th Panzer Division incorporated the 8th Panzer Brigade, composed of the 15th and 31st Panzer Regiment and was commanded by General-Lieutenant Heinrich Vietinghoff-Scheel. Panzer Abteilung 65, 66 and 67 were respectively assigned to the 1st, 2nd and 3rd Light Divisions.

In March 1939. Germany took over the remaining part of Czechoslovakia. Once again only a single unit was involved in the initial moves - this time the 3rd Panzer Division. Elements of the division reached Prague at 8.20 am on 13 March 1939; they were followed by the 6th Panzer Regiment which rolled in during the afternoon. On 15th March, the first parade of German tanks in Prague took place.

THE CZECH TANKS

Far more significant than the meagre forces obtained from the Anschluss were the armoured fighting vehicles which fell into German hands during the 1938/39 German takeover of the Czechoslovak state. Although, again, they were not strictly 'captured', and were simply handed over to the Germans. The two machines currently under Czech manufacture were to play a very significant role in the evolution of the Panzerwaffe. In due course the famous 8th Panzer Division would be equipped with Czech tanks. The two main Czechoslovak tanks were the Skoda / CKD LT-35 and CKD (also known as Praga and later as the B-LT-38, where the LT stood for Lehky Tank or Light Tank). The 38(t) had just begun its manufacturing cycle but 300 of the 35(t) were already available. Both were quickly pressed into German service as the Panzerkampfwagen 35(t) and 38(t) respectively. Although the LT-35 only remained in production until 1939 the LT-38 was manufactured until June 1942 under German supervision. The PzKpfw 35(t) served principally in the 1st Light Division until October 1939, when all were grouped into the 6th

Panzer Division. PzKpfw 38(t) saw service with various Light Divisions and was then used to equip various Panzer Divisions. By late 1941 the Germans at last had better tanks in production and the PzKpfw 35(t) and 38(t) were relegated to policing and security duties. Some PzKpfw 35(t) were exported and saw service with the Slovak and Bulgarian armies (where some actually served until the 1950s), others were used by the Romanian, Hungarian and Italian armies. The PzKpfw 38(t) was also exported and was in service with German Allies, including Romania. Slovakia, Bulgaria and Hungary. Both the PzKpfw 35(t) and the 38(t) saw extensive service in Poland, France and Russia. During the fighting in Russia, the need for heavier armour and armament soon made both Czech tanks redundant and they were swiftly relegated to reconnaissance duties. Overall, the Panzerkampfwagen 35(t) and 38(t) were reliable vehicles and served Panzertruppe very well in time of need.

ENTER WITTMANN

Among the new recruits at the time of the Czech takeover was a man who was to acquire legendary status in the ranks of the corps. His name was Michael Wittmann. Michael Wittman was born in the tiny village of Vogelthal, in the Upper Pfalz, on 22 April 1914. He was the first son of a farmer, Johann Wittmann, and his wife Ursula.

In 1934, at the age of 21, Wittmann joined the Germany army, signing up for a two-year tour. In the first days of the Nazi regime compulsory military service had not yet been reintroduced so Wittmann was a volunteer when he reported for military service in Freising, with the 19th Infantry Regiment. As a small standing army, comprised exclusively of volunteers, the inter-war Reichswehr was a high-quality force which expected very high standards. Wittman met those exacting standards and on the 1st November 1935, after one year in the service he was promoted to Grefreiter. The following year was the halcyon period for the Nazi party in Germany. The first flushes of economic successes for Hitler's National Socialists impressed the young Wittman. In the closed world of the military, the fervent Nazi beliefs of many of his colleagues also made an impression. Many of his colleagues planned to join the newly formed Waffen-SS and Wittmann decided that he, too, would join the military wing of the Nazi party after his own army service. On 1st November 1936 Wittmann applied for admission to the SS, and was accepted into what was to become one of the most notorious organisations in history.

In the case of many exceptional German soldiers, such as Field Marshall Erwin Rommel, supporters have subsequently tried to play down the enthusiasm they held for Hitler and all he stood for. This is not true of Michael Wittmann. In his case there was to be no redeeming conversion or late change of allegiance. He was a simple man and the seductive allure of the Nazi party drew his unquestioning obedience. Wittmann was given the SS number 311623 and proved to be a model National Socialist. In his free time he participated in sports, recruiting, and took part in the mass political demonstrations and

Michael Wittman was to become the most famous tank commander of World War II. His story is woven into the narrative of this book.

rallies of the period. Thanks to his rigorous military background. Wittmann met the very strict selection criteria and was accepted. He began training with his new unit on 5 April 1937, at the main cadet school in Berlin-Licherfelde. Wittmann was assigned to the 17th Company, which was an armoured scout car platoon. As part of an elite formation, the men of the armoured Scout Company received an intensive training course, which transformed them into expert soldiers.

These skills were later to stand him in good stead, but for the time being the new-found expertise was not needed. Hitler was still achieving his aims by a mixture of bluff and inspired gambles. In October 1938 Wittmann took part in the entry into the Sudetenland. The reception he witnessed as waves of excitement swept through the people made a lasting impression on him. The storm of jubilation eclipsed even the fervent national socialist rallies which he had attended. He was awarded his first of many medals, commemorating the reunification of Austria and the Sudetenland with the German Reich. From now on, medals and decorations would occupy a special place in Wittmann's affections.

TOWARDS THE CONFLAGRATION

The new Nazi regime was clearly not inclined to waste time. In the wake of the Czechoslovakian adventure, on 1 April 1939 the 10th Panzer Division (also known as 4th Panzer Brigade), commanded by General-Major Rudolf Schaal, began forming in Prague. In August/September 1939 an improvised Panzer Division Kempf (also known as Panzerverband Ostpreussen/Kempf) was raised. It was commanded by Werner Kempf. This division was made up of 7th Panzer Regiment along with various other units including SS Regiment 'Deutschland'.

In August 1939 there was a highly significant development. The production of tanks was clearly not keeping pace with the demands of the rapidly expanding Panzerwaffe, and the only solution was to reduce the number of tanks in a Panzer Division.

The strength of the Panzer Regiments within the Panzer Divisions was therefore revised. Each of the two Abteilungs was now composed of two light companies (equipped with the PzKpfw I and II) and one medium company (equipped with the PzKpfw III and IV) along with other units. Each Abteilung now had 71 to 74 tanks including 5 command tanks, and a regiment now boasted only 150 to 156 tanks including 12 command tanks. This meant a reduction in the strength of a Panzer Division from 570 machines to about 300. This was to prove an ominous portent for the future.

Each Panzer Division still had its own infantry, reconnaissance, artillery, transport, communication, medical, technical and general services component but the balance had already begun to shift. At that time 1st, 2nd and 3rd Panzer Divisions were identical in size and organisation, the 4th Panzer Division still lacked some infantry and anti-tank units, and the 5th Panzer Division had additional infantry and motorcycle units, making it the largest Panzer Division, while the 10th Panzer Division was not yet fully organised.

In 1939 Germany's rearmament was clearly far from complete, but if Hitler delayed his plans any longer Germany's enemies might then be too strong for her. To be successful he needed easy, quick and decisive victories; a great deal would therefore rest on the new Panzer formations. On 17 August 1939 all of the Panzer units were put on alert and prepared to move out. On 25th August, they began moving towards the eastern border of the Reich. On 1st September 1939 the Second World War began.

This photograph demonstrates the building of Sturmgeschütze and Panzer Mark IIIs side by side in the Alkett works in early 1941.

PANZERKAMPFWAGEN II SD.KFZ.121

With suspension developed from the Panzer I, the Panzer II was a larger vehicle but still only intended as a light training tank. It entered service only because the development of the more efficient PzKpfw IIIs and IVs was delayed and a larger, gun armed vehicle was needed. The chassis was designed by MAN and the Panzer II went into production in 1935. The first variants of the Panzer II consisted of Ausf al, a2 and a3 which had small modifications of the engine and cooling system.

The Ausf C became the main production prototype of the Panzer II. With a new suspension (five separate roadwheels) the Ausf C were thereafter used not only as the lead combat tank, but also as training tanks.

In May 1938 the Ausf D/E, the Schnellkampfwagen, appeared bringing another new suspension: the Famo/Christie-type. However, this proved rather unsuccessful and the Ausf D/E was taken out of service after an unsatisfactory performance. The Ausf C continued to receive modifications and between 1940 and 1943 versions of this -Aust F and G -were introduced.

The Panzer II was used in large numbers by the Panzertruppe during Polish and French campaigns and later saw extensive service with Erwin Rommel's DAK in North Africa and in the opening stages of the Russian Campaign. One source reports that by the French campaign of 1940, 955 Panzer II were in the hands of the Wehrmacht. Although they were undoubtedly fast vehicles, the PzKpfw II suffered from very thin armour, which offered minimal protection in battle, and an inadequate 20mm gun.

The Panzer II had room for one extra crew man which made the vehicles slightly more efficient, but there were still far too few to handle all the tasks faced by a crew in combat.

Armour (mm/angle) Ausf A/B/C Sd. Kfz. 121	Armour (mm/angle) Ausf L (Luchs) Sd. Kfz. 123
Front Turret: 14.5/round	Front Turret: 30/10
Front Upper Hull: 14.5/9	Front Upper Hull: 30/10
Front Lower Hull: 14.5/round	Front Lower Hull: 30/22
Side Turret: 14.5/22	Side Turret: 20/21
Side Upper Hull: 14.5/0	Side Upper Hull: 20/0
Side Lower Hull: 14.5/0	Side Lower Hull: 20/0
Rear Turret: 14.5/22	Rear Turret: 20/21
Rear Upper Hull: 14.5/9	Rear Upper Hull: 20/28
Rear Lower Hull: 14.5/6	Rear Lower Hull: 20/28
Turret Top/ Bottom: 10/86	Turret Top / Bottom: 12/79
Upper Hull Top / Bottom: 10/81	Upper Hull Top / Bottom: 10/86
Lower Hull Top / Bottom: 14.5/73 5/90	Lower Hull Tip / Bottom: 10/90
Gun Mantlet: 16/round	Gun Mantlet: 30/round

Model	Ausf A/B/C Sd. Kfz. 121	Ausf L (Luchs) Sd. Kfz. 123
Weight	9500 kg	11800 kg
Crew	3	4
Engine	Maybach HL 62 TRM 6-cylinder / 140hp	Maybach HL 66 P 6-cylinder / 180hp
Speed	Road: 40 km/h	Road: 60km/h
Range	Road: 200 km Crosscountry: 125 km	Road: 290 km Crosscountry: 175 km
Fuel Capacity	170 litres	235 litres
Length	4.81 m	4.63 m
Width	2.28 m	2.48 m
Height	2.02 m	2.21 m
Armament	20mm Kwk 30 or 38 L/55 & 1 x 7.92mm MG34 (1 x MG-coax)	20mm Kwk 38 L/55 1 x 7.92mm MG34 (1 x MG-hull)
Ammunition Supply	20mm - 180 rounds 7.92 - 3525 rounds	20mm - 320 rounds 7.92 - 2280 rounds

Model	Production Period	Number Of Chassis Produced	Number Of Pz. Kpfw. II Produced
Ausf a1	Late May 1935 - May 1936	10	75
Ausf a2	May 1936 - February 1937	25	
Ausf a3	May 1936 - February 1937	50	
Ausf b	February - March 1937	25	25
Ausf c	1937	1900	1113
Ausf A	1938-40	1000	
Ausf B	1938-40	2000	
Ausf C	1938-40	1000	
Ausf D	1938-41	800	43
Ausf E	1938-41	200	
Ausf F	1940-43	1400	524
Ausf G1/G3/G4 (nA) (VK 901)	April 1941 - February 1942	75 (12 completed)	12
Ausf H (nA verst) (VK 903)	September 1941	1 prototype	-
Ausf J (nA verst) (VK 1601)	April - December 1942	22 - 25	22
Leopard (VK 901)	March 1942 - January 1943	1 prototype incomplete	-
Ausf M (nA verst) (VK 1301)	August 1942	4	4
Ausf L (Luchs) (VK 1301)	September 1943 - January 1944	104	104

The 20mm gun of the Panzer II was patently unsuited to the challenge of a modern battlefield, but delays with the introduction of the Panzer III and IV meant that this training tank would see front line service.

CONVERSIONS

- **Marder II (Sd.Kfz.l32)**
- **Marder II (Sd.Kfz.l31)**
- **Wespe (Sd. Kfz. 124)** - 105mm light field howitzer carrier
- **Sturmpanzer II Bison** - 150mm sIG 33 gun carrier
- **Beobachtungswagen II Ausf C** - post/command vehicle
- **Munitionsschlepper II** - ammunition carrier
- **PzKfw (Flammpanzer) II Flamingo (Sd. Kfz. 122) (AusfD/E)**
- **Brueckenleger auf PzKpfw 11 Ausf b** - light bridging vehicle (1+ produced in 1939)
- **Panzerspahwagen II Ausf L Luchs** - reconnaissance tank
- **Schwimm Panzer II Ausf. A-C (20mm gun)** - amphibious tank (52 converted)
- **Bergepanzer II Ausf D/E** - recovery vehicle
- **Ladungsleger II** - explosive charge layer
- **Panzer Beobachtungswagen II** - artillery observation tank
- **Pioner-Kampfwagen II** - engineer vehicle
- **PzKpfw II AusfA/B/C armed with 50mm Pak 38 L/60 gun**
- **Feuerleitpanzer II** - fire directing tank

TACTICS AND LOGISTICS

"At the present time, due to our lack of practical experience, any thoughts on the equipping and organisation of Panzer units may only be based on theory. A close study should be made of countries which have practical experience without the encumbrances we have endured in the fifteen years since the war."

GENERAL BECK GENERALSTABES DES HEERES, 1936

The training given to the Panzer warriors emphasised speed and independence of thought. When these units were unleashed they offered a very effective weapon that their enemies found impossible to fight against. In Poland this new force had the first opportunity to put its meticulous training into practice; the campaign was a triumph for the Wehrmacht and showed the potential for the tank in battle. Nonetheless, some problems were encountered.

'*...In general the bravery and heroism of the Polish Army merits great respect*', said Generalfeldmarshall Gerd von Rundstedt.

It was here that the ideas of General Heinz Guderian came to appear increasingly attractive. A man of acute intelligence, his plans and tactics were tried out in war games and manoeuvres; once they proved successful in practice they soon convinced Germany's dictator that he had discovered the way to make his dream become a reality. Every detail of the organisation of the Panzer Divisions was explored in meticulous detail so that nothing was left to chance.

The 'Victory in the West' exhibition staged in Vienna during 1941. This startling achievement was largely due to the efficient employment of the German tank forces. The victory exhibition was designed to underline the effectiveness of the new German military machine.

MOVEMENT ORDERS

The movement of the Panzer Division was a difficult undertaking and was the subject of scrutiny and careful consideration. For a smooth functioning of the march the Germans stressed: systematic training and practice; attention to detail; care of vehicles and equipment; advanced reconnaissance of routes; precise warning orders; and the issue of detailed march orders. Worked out during the brief adolescence of the Panzer Divisions from 1935-1939, these careful plans were to be rewarded with many successes in the years to come.

In order to secure the march column against enemy attacks, the Germans divided the Panzer column into an Advance Guard (Vorhut), Main Body (Gros), and Rear Guard (Nachhut).

The issue of orders for march and traffic control was the responsibility of the higher command. Movement by road of formations from battalion strength upwards was carried out in the Zone of the Interior at the orders of the Army High Command (OKH) or a headquarters acting on the orders of the Army High Command. In the theatre of war these movements were strictly controlled by Army Headquarters, which issued orders in accordance with instructions from Army High Command or the Army Group. Movements in the areas of military commanders of line-of-communication areas were controlled by orders of the commanders of the relevant areas.

Orders for movement were issued to the formations of fighting troops by the operations group headquarters; those to supply services and units in the line-of-communication area emanated from the supply and administrative group.

The Germans set up a well-organised traffic control service which came under the orders of the operations group. All traffic control services usually wore orange-red brassards. The members of the military police, distinguished by their metal gorgets, also made themselves highly visible to ensure the smooth flow of vehicles.

The Germans allotted to each front line division its own road or sector of advance, usually marked by advance parties. General Headquarters or any other troops directed simultaneously on the same roads were subordinated to the division for the duration of the move. All-weather roads were usually allotted to motorised or armoured divisions, while subsidiary roads were assigned to infantry divisions. Of course Guderian's work was not merely limited to logistics and movement. The real thought was applied to how these new formations could be used in action.

OPERATIONAL PRINCIPLES

In 1945 the US army intelligence section compiled a manual for US troops going to fight in France. This detailed work gives us a fascinating glimpse into the Wehrmacht of 1945 as viewed through allied eyes. One particularly noteworthy section concentrates on German battle tactics. Although the manual was designed for the forces in 1945, these were the same operational principles which were drilled into the Panzertruppen in 1939. It is worth reporting a lengthy sequence here, as the overall objectives of the employment of armoured forces in World War II is well explained:

"The fundamental principle of German offensive doctrine is to encircle and destroy the enemy. The objective of the combined arms in attack is to bring the armoured forces and the infantry into decisive action against the enemy with sufficient firepower and shock. Superiority in force and firepower, the employment of armoured forces, as well as the surprise element, play a great part in the offensive.

Co-ordination between the combined arms under a strong unified command is, the Germans emphasise, an absolute requisite of these shock tactics. This has become more and more true as the Allies have developed effective anti-tank weapons and have adapted deeper defences, limiting the self-sufficiency of German tanks. To counter these measures the Germans have increased the mobility and armour protection of their motor-borne infantry, and have mounted a large proportion of both their direct and indirect heavy support weapons on self-propelled carriages.

In attempting thoroughly to paralyse the defender up to the moment of the tank-infantry assault the Germans realise that even the most formidable forces are never sufficient for overwhelming superiority on the entire front. They therefore select a point of main effort (Schwerpunkt) for a breakthrough, allotting narrow sectors of attack (Gefechtsstreifen) to the troops committed at the decisive locality. There they also mass the bulk of their heavy weapons and reserves. The other sectors of the front are engaged by weaker, diversionary forces. In selecting the point of main effort, the Germans consider weaknesses in the enemy's defensive position; suitability of the terrain, especially for tanks and for co-operation of all arms: approach routes: and possibilities for supporting fire, especially artillery. Although the Germans select a point of main effort in all attacks they usually also make plans for shifting their main effort if they meet unexpected success elsewhere. To allow such shifts, sufficient reserves and a strong, unified command are organised.

An attack on a narrow front, according to German doctrine, must have sufficient forces at its disposal to widen the penetration while maintaining its impetus, and to protect the flanks of the penetration. Once the attack is launched, it must drive straight to its objective, regardless of opposition.

MAIN TYPES OF ATTACK

THE FLANK ATTACK (*Flankenangriff*)
The Germans consider that the most effective attack is against the enemy's flank. The flank attack develops either from the approach march -sometimes through a turning movement - or from flank marches. It attempts to surprise the enemy and permit him no time for countermeasures. Since mobility and the deception of the enemy at other positions are required, the flank attack is most successfully mounted from a distance; the troop movements necessary for the manoeuvre can be executed in close proximity to the enemy only with unusually favourable terrain or at night. Attacks are launched on both flanks only when the Germans consider their forces clearly superior.

The Panzer IV (F2) with the short barrelled 75mm infantry support gun.

ENVELOPMENT *(Umfassungsangriff)*

The envelopment is a combination flank-and-frontal attack especially favoured by the Germans. The envelopment may be directed on either or both the enemy's flanks, and is accompanied by a simultaneous frontal attack to fix the enemy's forces. The deeper the envelopment goes into the enemy's flanks, the greater becomes the danger of being enveloped oneself. The Germans therefore emphasise the necessity of strong reserves and organisation of the enveloping forces in depth. Success of the envelopment depends on the extent to which the enemy is able to dispose his forces in the threatened direction.

ENCIRCLEMENT *(Einkreisung)*

An encirclement, the Germans think, is a particularly decisive form of attack, but usually more difficult to execute than a flank attack or an envelopment. In an encirclement the enemy is not attacked at all in front, or is attacked in front only by light forces, while the main attacking force passes entirely around him, with the objective of manoeuvring him out of position. This requires extreme mobility and deception.

FRONTAL ATTACK *(Frontalangriff)*

The Germans consider the frontal attack the most difficult of execution. It strikes the enemy at his strongest point, and therefore requires superiority of men and material. A frontal attack should be made only at a point where the infantry can break through into favourable terrain in the depth of the enemy position. The frontage of the attack should be wider than the actual area (Schwerpunkt) chosen for penetration, in order to tie down the enemy on the flanks of the breakthrough. Adequate reserves must be held ready to counter the employment of the enemy's reserves.

WING ATTACK *(Flugelangriff)*

An attack directed at one or both of the enemy's wings has, the Germans teach, a better chance of success than a central frontal attack, since only a part of the enemy's weapons are faced, and only one flank of the attacking force or forces is exposed to enemy fire. Bending back one wing may give an opportunity for a flank attack, or for a single or double envelopment.

PENETRATION AND BREAKTHROUGH *(Einbruch und Durchbruch).*

These are not separate forms of attack, but, rather, the exploitation of a successful attack on the enemy's front, wing or flank. The penetration destroys the continuity of the hostile front. The broader the penetration, the deeper the penetration wedge can be driven. Strong reserves throw back enemy counter-attack against the flanks of the penetration. German units are trained to exploit a penetration to the maximum so that it may develop into a complete breakthrough before hostile counter-measures can be launched on an effective scale. The deeper the attacker penetrates, the more effectively can he envelop and frustrate the attempts of the enemy to close his front again by withdrawal to the rear. The attacking forces attempt to reduce individual enemy positions by encircling and isolating them. The Germans do not consider a breakthrough successful until they overcome the enemy's artillery positions, which is usually the special task of tanks. Reserve units roll up the enemy's front from the newly created flanks.

ATTACKS BY MECHANISED FORCES

In armoured-force operations, the Germans stress the need for the concentrated employment, at the decisive place and time, of the entire combined command of tanks and other arms, less necessary reserves. The tanks constitute the striking force of such a command and normally advance as the first echelon of the attack. Their primary mission is to break through and attack the enemy artillery, rather than to seek out and destroy enemy tanks, which can be more effectively engaged by anti-tank units. The mission of the other arms is to assist the

A powerful study of a Panzer III involved in street fighting for Shitomir during August 1941. The warning not to take tank into cities was ignored time and time again. Every time they did so the Panzerwaffe paid a high price.

tanks in their advance, and particularly to eliminate anti-tank weapons. The smallest combat unit in such a force of combined arms is the company.

The basic formation for the tank platoon, company, and battalion are file, double file, wedge and blunt wedge. The type of formation used for a specific task depends to a large extent on terrain conditions and the strength of enemy opposition. A German tank platoon normally consists of one command tank and two tank squads of two tanks each.

The tank regiment normally attacks in waves, in either of the following manners. The tank regiment is echeloned in depth, one tank battalion following the other. The regimental commander's location is between the two battalions. This formation has the advantages of a sufficiently wide front (about one thousand one hundred yards), and close contact by the commander of his units in the conduct of the attack. The normal depth of such a formation is about three thousand yards. This is the usual form of the tank attack. When two tank battalions are attacking, one behind the other, it takes them about half an hour to pass their own infantry.

When the two-battalions-abreast formation is employed, it almost essential that another tank regiment form the following wave. This formation usually has the disadvantage of being too wide. The regimental commander cannot observe his units, and he has no units of his own behind him which he can commit in a decisive moment. The attack normally proceeds in three waves.

The first wave thrusts to the enemy's anti-tank defence and artillery positions.

The second wave provides covering fire for the first wave, and then attacks the enemy's infantry positions, preceded, accompanied or followed by part of the Panzer grenadiers, who dismount as close as possible to the point where they must engage the enemy. The objectives of the second wave are the remaining anti-tank positions of heavy infantry-support weapons, and machine gun emplacements which hold up the advance of the infantry.

The third wave, accompanied by the remainder of the Panzer grenadiers, mops up.

These three waves are now often telescoped into two, the first wave speeding through the enemy's position as far as his gun positions, the second crushing the enemy's forward positions in detail and mopping up the opposition not dealt with by the first wave or which has revived since the first

A typical attack formation of this type might be divided up among the Panzer division's units as follows: the first wave, on a frontage of about two thousand to three thousand yards, might consist of one tank battalion, two companies forward, supported on the flanks by elements of the assault gun battalion. Close to the rear of the first wave usually follow one or two Panzer grenadier companies in armoured half-trucks. About one hundred and fifty yards to the rear of the first wave moves the second wave, formed of the second tank battalion in the same formation, closely followed by the remainder of the armoured Panzer grenadiers, who are in turn followed at some distance by the motorised Panzer grenadiers. The flanks are protected by anti-tank guns which are normally operated by platoons, moving by bounds. The artillery forward observer travels in his armoured vehicles with the first wave, while the artillery commander of the supporting artillery units usually travels with the tank commander. Assault guns normally also accompany the second wave.

The tanks help each other forward by fire and movement, medium or heavy tanks taking up hull-down firing positions and giving covering fire while the faster tanks advance to the next commanding feature. Then, the latter give covering fire to the former moving forward to their next bound.

Once the first wave has reached the rear of the enemy's forward defences, it pushes straight on to attack the enemy's artillery. As soon as these positions have been neutralised, the tanks reform beyond the artillery positions and either prepare to exploit the attack or form an all-round defensive position on suitable ground.

The tank unit commander, as the leader of the strongest unit, is in most cases in command of the combat team, and all the other participating arms (Panzer grenadiers, artillery, engineers and anti-tank units) are placed under him. The Germans realise that a strong and unified command is an essential feature of any military operation. For certain missions, however, tank units are attached to another arm, in which case the tank commander is consulted before the final plans for the operations are made.

INFANTRY TANK CO-OPERATION

When the enemy has well prepared positions with natural or constructed tank obstacles, the German infantry attacks before the tanks and clears the way. The objective of the infantry is to penetrate into the enemy position and destroy enemy anti-tank weapons to the limit of its strength and the fire power of its own support weapons, augmented by additional support and covering fire from the tanks and self-propelled weapons sited in their rear.

Only after the destruction of the enemy anti-tank defence can the tanks be employed on the battle line to the fullest advantage.

When the tank obstacles in front of the enemy position are already destroyed, and no additional tank obstacles are expected in the depth the enemy's main defensive position, the infantry breaks through simultaneously with the tank unit. The infantry attack is conducted in the same manner as it would be without the co-operation of tanks. Heavy infantry weapons are kept in readiness to fire at possible newly discovered anti-tank positions. Of particular importance is protection of the open flanks by echeloning the flank units and employing heavy weapons at the flanks.

In most cases, the infantry follows the tanks closely, taking advantage of the firepower and paralysing effect of the tanks upon the enemy's defence. The Germans normally transport the infantry to the line of departure on tanks or troop-carrying vehicles in order to protect the infantry and to increase its speed. The infantry leaves the vehicles at the last possible moment, and goes into action mainly with light automatic weapons.

A Panzer II fords a river during the advance in Greece.

One of a remarkable sequence of pictures illustrating General Heinz Guderian at the front. It was Guderian's vision which had led to the creation of the Panzerwaffe and he now demonstrated a masterful ability in the field.

The tanks advance by bounds from cover to cover, reconnoitring the terrain ahead and providing protective fire for the dismounted Panzer grenadiers. The tanks do not slow their advance to enable the infantry to keep continuous pace with them, but advance alone and wait under cover until the infantry catches up with the advance, terrain that does not offer sufficient cover is crossed with the greatest possible speed.

The infantry attacks in small formations also by bounds under the fire cover of its own heavy weapons and of the tanks, staying away from individual tanks because they draw the strongest enemy fire.

When a tank company attacks with infantry, there are normally two platoons on the line, one platoon back, and the fourth platoon in reserve. The interval between tanks is usually 100 to 120 yards.

The tank's machine guns usually engage infantry targets at about one thousand yards range and under, while the tank guns engage targets at 2000-2500 yards.

The co-ordination between tanks and Panzer grenadiers moving into combat on armoured half-tracks is similar to the technique employed in a purely armoured formation, since the armoured half-tracks are not only troop carrying vehicles but also combat vehicles. When the terrain is favourable for tank warfare, Panzer grenadiers in their armoured half-tracks follow immediately with the second wave, after the first tank wave has overrun the opponent's position. A deep and narrow formation is employed. After the penetration, the main mission of the Panzer grenadiers is to overcome the enemy positions which survived the first wave.

In attacking enemy pillboxes the Germans use combat groups consisting of tank's, infantry and engineers, assisted by artillery. The normal composition of a combat group attacking line bunker is one platoon of tanks and one platoon of infantry reinforced by one squad of engineers. Before the combat group is committed against the enemy pillbox, artillery fires high explosives and smoke shells at the neighbouring pillboxes to isolate them, shells the terrain between pillboxes, and conducts counter-battery fire. Under the protection of this fire, the combat group advances close to the pillbox while other infantry units attack the enemy in the terrain between the pillboxes.

One tank squad covers the advances of the other tank squads and the infantry platoon by direct fire against the pillbox, particularly against the observation and weapons openings. The first tank squad halts under cover whenever possible and covers the advance of the second tank squad.

GUN AND AMMUNITION NOMENCLATURE

During World War II the Wehrmacht generally described small arms such as pistols and machine guns by the diameter of their bore in millimetres, the most common being 7.92 mm and 9mm. Larger calibre guns were usually categorised in centimetres. The practice in most countries was also to use millimetres, for example the American 75 mm M3. British tanks and anti-tank guns and some artillery pieces were differentiated by the weight of the projectile they fired, for example the 6-pounder and 17-pounder. However, some older British types retained their identification by the diameter of their bore in inches. 'Calibre' refers to the diameter of the barrel, usually omitting the rifling. We refer to a 7.92 mm-calibre MG34 medium machine gun. Small arms ammunition was frequently known by its calibre and cartridge length together, 7.92 mm x 57, or by attaching a common name to the calibre, such as Parabellum or ACP. These rules were not applied in any hard or fast manner and variations can be endless.

With the artillery the term calibre was used to describe the diameter of the bore of a gun's barrel in relation to the length of the barrel. The Americans measure this length from the back of the chamber to the muzzle and the Germans measure from the back of the breech to the muzzle, therefore a gun of 56 calibres - often symbolized as L/56 - has a barrel 56 times the length of its nominal bore. In the case of the German KwK 36 8.8 cm L/56 gun, this means a total barrel length of 56 x 8.8 cm, or 4.93 m.

Rifle and machine-gun calibre ammunition came in many shapes, including incendiary and explosive types. The most common were the jacketed hard point (JHP), jacketed soft point (JSP), tracer and armour-piercing (AP). For the Tiger, three types of 8.8 cm ammunition were dispensed - armour-piercing, high explosive (HE) and high-explosive anti-tank (HEAT). The customary variety of armour-piercing was the Pzgr.39, a 10.2 kg armour-piercing capped, ballistic-capped round with an explosive centre which left the KwK36's muzzle at a velocity of 773 m/sec.

AP rounds usually accounted for half of a Tiger's ammunition supply, the rest taken up with Sprgr. HE rounds for use against soft-skinned vehicles. The hollow-charge Gr.39HL round, which was less productive at short range, was sometimes exchanged for some of the HE load despite being less accurate. The Pzgr.39 APCBC round was capable of piercing 120 mm of armour at an angle of 30 degrees within a range of 1000 m. The tungsten-cored Pzgr.40 round could easily pierce 170 mm of armour at short range and 110 mm at 2000 m, while the Gr.39HL round could penetrate 90 mm of armour up to 2000 m.

The nightmare for every tank crew was to have to dismount the vehicle and change tracks under enemy fire. This was an alarmingly frequent occurrence; nonetheless every effort had to be made to salvage an immobilised vehicle. (Propaganda drawing from Signal Magazine).

When the combat group reaches the barbed wire obstacle surrounding the pillbox, the two tank squads have different missions. One tank squad remains in front of the pillbox, and its tanks are driven into a position from which they can overlook the terrain, and watch out for anti-tank guns and machine gun emplacements, while the other tank squad (the pillbox tank squad) rolls across the obstacle to enable the infantry and engineers to get close to the pillbox. The pillbox tank squad then fires on the pillbox at close range. The infantry squad meanwhile takes the surrounding terrain and covers the engineers who blast the entrance of the pillbox with TNT.

ARTILLERY-TANK CO-ORDINATION

Artillery support is of decisive importance for the preparation and the successful conduct of a tank attack. A unified command for the entire artillery controls the artillery fire as long as the infantry and tank units are fighting on the same line. When the tanks break through the enemy forward defence lines, the self-propelled artillery or any other artillery battalion designated for the support of the tank unit is placed under the command of the tank unit commander.

The Germans believe that the artillery fire must not check the momentum of the attack. Consequently the heaviest fire must fall well ahead of the tanks or outside their sector.

The mission of the artillery preparation before the attack is to destroy, or at least to neutralise, the opponent's anti-tank defence in the area between the line of contact and the regimental reserve line. Continuous counter-battery fire prevents the enemy from shelling the tank assembly area and from breaking up the preparation of the tank attack.

The artillery has the following missions before the tank attack:

Counter-battery fire on enemy artillery located in positions which command the ground over which the tank attack is to be made.

Concentrations on enemy tanks in assembly areas:

Harassing fire on all areas in which the anti-tank units are located or suspected. Fire is heaviest on areas in which tanks cannot operate but from which they can be engaged effectively.

Adjusting fire with high explosives on probable enemy observation posts commanding the sector to be attacked. These observation posts are blinded with smoke as soon as the attack begins.

Experience has taught the Germans that the flanks of a tank attack are vulnerable. Therefore they assign to the artillery and the rocket projector units the task of protecting flanks by barrages using high explosives and smoke shells.

The artillery has the following missions during the tank attack:

Counter-battery fire.

Blinding enemy observation posts.

As the attack progresses, engaging successive lines of anti-tank defence, especially areas to the rear and flanks of the sector attacked.

Screening the flanks of the attack with smoke and neutralising the enemy's infantry and rear areas.

Delaying the movement and deployment of enemy reserves, particularly tanks

The Germans stress that this wide variety of tasks must not lead to the wholesale dispersal of effort. The main task of the artillery is at all times the destruction of the enemy's anti-tank weapons, tanks, and artillery.

Liaison between artillery and tanks during the attack is established by the commanding officers and the artillery liaison group, which normally moves with the first wave. Artillery forward observers, if possible in armoured observation posts, ride with the most forward elements. A German field expedient is for the tank unit to take along a forward observer in one of its tanks. It often happens that the tank man himself has to take over the observation for the artillery. He himself can request artillery fire and shift concentrations when the situation requires such changes."

INSIDE THE PANZERS

To the infantrymen crouched in their foxholes, even the smallest tanks project an aura of invincibility. Rolling relentlessly onwards, they can seem like an unstoppable armoured juggernaut, the very essence of armoured might. Tanks appear from the outside to be so invulnerable and impersonal, it's easy to forget that, inside the vehicle, there are men just the same as any others, with the same fears and emotions which run through every soldier on the battlefield.

In many respects, these emotions are heightened because the tank gives the protection of its armour, but imposes a host of other restrictions on its crew.

Inside the tank, visibility is severely limited. The interior is cramped and noisy. The crew are acutely aware that their vehicle is a prime target for every enemy weapon on the battlefield. With their own stocks of fuel and ammunition aboard, they know that one hit can turn the tank into a blazing inferno. There is also the danger that infantrymen might get close enough to attack with anti-tank weapons, from unseen hiding places.

The main source of danger for tank crews in battle during the Second World War stemmed chiefly from the lack of visibility from inside the tank. The crew relied on a series of narrow vision slits that allowed them to see a very small area directly in front of that slit; the early Panzers had a number of those around the vehicles but there were always blind spots. Most armour on the battlefield at that time didn't move much quicker than a man running; in consequence a man running with a hand-held anti-tank device was frequently able to out-manoeuvre tanks.

Shortly after the Second World War Basil Liddel-Hart conducted a highly impressive series of interviews with leading German officers which formed the basis for a masterful study entitled The Other Side of the Hill. From the ranks of the Panzerwaffe Liddell personally interviewed Guderian, von Thoma and Manteuffel - who was to rise to prominence later in the war.

One factor which emerged very clearly from those discussions was the reliance on the speed of armour as opposed to the heaviness of its ordnance or armour plate. Manteuffel went as far as to

Assembly workers hard at work producing Sturmgeschtze in January 1942. These machines are equipped with the short-barrelled 75mm which had already proven to be ineffective for many of the tasks faced by the Stug.

stress that the speed of manoeuvrability of a tank was by far the most important attribute. Von Thoma confirmed this view when he asserted that, given the choice between a thick skin or a fast runner, he would choose the fast runner every time. This view made for an interesting departure from the commonly held view that the German High Command valued heavy tanks above all else.

Under favourable circumstances, placed in good positions, with their strong frontal armour facing the enemy the crews of the German tanks of the Second World War had good cause for confidence. The Panthers and Tigers of the later war years could withstand most guns on the battlefield from all but the closest ranges. Once infantry tank-hunting teams got close to the tanks, or enemy tanks were able to manoeuvre into a position to fire at the weaker sides or rear of the tank, the picture changed dramatically. The all conquering armoured hull could just as soon turn into a steel coffin.

For tank commanders to have a good field of vision, it was necessary for them to stand with their heads fully exposed outside the vehicle. But when the bullets started to fly, the commander and driver had to retreat inside the vehicle, closing their hatches behind them. Once the tank was battened down, the crew had only a very limited view of the outside world. With their diesel engines roaring and weapons firing, the heat generated inside the tanks was oppressive. In battle, the noise, the smell of sweat, smoke, fear and cordite, was an ever-present ingredient to life in the Panzers. Not only was it a claustrophobic world, unbearably noisy and uncomfortably cramped, but the severely restricted view made it difficult to spot targets or to defend against enemy tank-hunting teams.

Once the tank was battened down for better protection it became difficult to see anything at all, especially for the driver, who only had very small slots to look through and he could see very little. He had to rely on the commander to a great deal, who was sitting higher up in the tank, to advise him if there was any trouble ahead. In the Second World War tank-hunting teams were trained to move up close to enemy tanks to disable them. Occasionally they would climb onto vehicles themselves and set anti-tank mines or drop grenades into exhaust outlets and any open hatches.

As it was designed to fire over long ranges, the main gun of the tank was useless at close quarters. For combat against infantrymen who got too near the vehicle, tanks were equipped with grenade dischargers which could be operated from inside. The turret of a tank is very much like a mobile pillbox, with only the minimal openings for weapons. The armour gives protection, but severely limits visibility. In desperate situations there was the option of a small opening called a pistol port. When teams of infantry got close enough to climb onto the vehicles themselves, the crew of the tank had to either clamber out and engage the enemy with small arms, or rely on supporting infantry and other tanks in the unit to spray their vehicle with machine gun fire to kill any infantry clambering aboard.

Tanks of all nations tended to mount at least one or two machine guns for close quarter defence. Some tanks in fact mounted as many as six. But in addition to these, smoke projectors which could lay a smoke screen, mine layers, grenade launchers and even light mortars could be built on to tanks for close quarter protection against infantry or anti-tank gun crews. Later in the war the Germans used a cement-like paste called Zimmerit which coated the sides of the vehicles that were reachable by anyone attacking the tank; its purpose being to stop magnetic mines being attached. At longer ranges, there were other dangers. Concealed anti-tank guns were the chief menace. One well-placed shot could blast a tank to fragments. These guns were difficult to spot and could be camouflaged very easily.

In order to give the tanks protection against enemy guns they need as much armour as possible. Ideally, every inch would be covered in thick steel plate. However, the crew need to be able to see out of a tank, so vision slits and hatches had to be allowed for. The engines need air intakes, and exhaust pipes to allow the fumes to escape from the engine. These weakly armoured parts of the tank are where it is most vulnerable, and they were the favourite aiming points for lurking anti-tank guns. From the confines of a tank, anti-tank guns were often impossible to find until it was too late.

COMMUNICATIONS

With the high levels of noise inside a Panzer communication was very difficult. To communicate with other vehicles, other than by radio, was almost impossible.

The German engineers solved the problem of internal communications by an internal intercom which linked the crew and allowed them to communicate via headphones and microphones. The German practice at the time was to use a throat microphone which had two small microphones against the side of the throat; these would be pressed to speak to the rest of the crew. The radio set over that also allowed for broadcasts to the rest of the unit. The headset had a pair of headphones to muffle the sound of the engine but it generally was a very loud engine anyway. For communications between the tanks themselves, all German machines were equipped with radios. In the early war years, there were no such refinements on the Russian side.

In the famous T-34 for example, as good as the tank was, the communication was very poor. Early models had no radio at all so the commander had to get out of his turret and wave two flags about, one red and one green, and give signals like a ship on the high seas. This primitive system had initially been used by the Panzerwaffe, who of course discovered that it did not work very well. It was only much later that the T-34/85 had a proper radio for contact with each crew member and of course to Headquarters.

AMMUNITION

With the space taken up by the main gun, the crew and the engines, there was surprisingly little room in a tank for the ammunition which was vital to survival on the battlefield. Most tanks could hold enough shells for around ninety shots, tightly packed into every conceivable space. Most commanders favoured a mix of 40 per cent high explosive and 60 per cent armour piercing, but it was often a matter of a personal assessment of the likeliest target to be faced on a given mission. Getting the balance right was a crucial decision. Armour piercing rounds were useless against infantry and high explosive would not penetrate tank armour. Having a large stock of the wrong kind of ammunition effectively left the tank impotent.

In battle, many experienced crews could fire one round every five seconds, so not surprisingly, ammunition supplies could quickly become exhausted, rendering the tank helpless. At this delicate juncture, the tank commander was faced with a crucial choice: either leave the field to re-arm and re-fuel, or await re-supply in the field.

A hurried field conference, as the men of the leading tanks in a German formation threatening Dubno are briefed on their next mission.

The bulky tank ammunition could not be transported on foot and required a vehicle to re-supply the tanks. Trucks were too vulnerable to be sent into the fighting area, so the Germans developed a special turretless tank called a Munition-schlepper to carry out the dangerous job of ammunition re-supply on the battlefield.

To ensure that ammunition supplies were used wisely. German tanks were forbidden from firing on the move. The prescribed tactic was to strictly engage enemy targets from a static position. This made aiming much easier giving the gunner the best chance as he lined up his target on the middle triangle of his gun sight. To help him in aiming his shells, they were equipped with a tracer element, which produced a trail of bright light to help pinpoint the path of the shell as it flew towards its target.

PANZERKAMPFWAGEN III SD.KFZ.141

The PzKpfw III was designed to be the Wehrmacht's main combat machine and was developed by Daimler-Benz in the mid 1930s under the pseudonym Zugfuhrerwagen, which means platoon commanders' truck. The first prototype of the PzKpfw III was produced by Daimler-Benz in Berlin 1936. As the introduction of a 50mm gun would have meant a considerable re-design, the 37mm gun was used instead.

Following numerous modifications, the Ausf A (1-Serie) appeared in May 1937 and : by the end of 1937, 15 were produced. Only 8 of the Ausf As were fully armed and the unarmed machines were used for further testing and modification.

Daimler-Benz produced 15 Ausf Bs (2-Serie) in 1937, 15 Ausf Cs (3a-Serie) by the beginning of 1938; it continued by introducing the next variant the Ausf D (3b-Serie), 55 of which were produced in 1939. Of the entire Ausf Ds production run, only 30 were armed.

All early models of the Panzer HI, including the Ausf A/B/C/D were pre-prototypes of the whole series and were unsuitable for large scale production. Every new prototype was a marginal improvement on the last. Each model featured a different type of suspension, a variation on the Maybach DSO -such as the HL 108 TR engine. Only a relatively few vehicles saw combat in the early stages of the war; the Ausf D saw service during fighting in Denmark and Norway in May 1940 and in Finland in 1941/42. In February 1940,

A pair of Panzer III tanks stand guard in a recently captured French town.

remaining Panzer IIIs Ausf D were handed over to NSKK for training purposes.

The first Panzer III model to go into anything like full-scale production was the Ausf E of which 96 were produced. With a thicker 30mm frontal armour, a Maybach HL 120TR engine and new suspension and gearbox putting its weight up to 19.5 tonnes, the Ausf E was the best machine so far.

By 1940, and during the 'E' model production, it was decided to fit all models with a 50mm gun as standard. The L/42 gun was fitted on Ausf E, F, G and H. From 1941, Hitler insisted that the more powerful L/60 (50mm) gun was fitted on Ausf J-1. In 1942, 104 Ausf J's were converted to Panzerbefehlswagen III and in April 1943, 100 Ausf M's were converted by Wegmann into the Flammpanzer (Flamethrower Tank); designed to fight in urban areas such as Stalingrad. Although the models produced never actually reached Stalingrad they did see service on the Eastern Front. Additionally, many Ausf Ms were converted into the Sturmgeschütz III or the Ausf N.

The Panzer III provided the main battle tank for the Panzer Divisions in the early years of the war. Yet its production was slow and stopped altogether in August 1943.

However, in 1943/44, the Panzer III prototypes were fitted with dozers and were used to clean up the streets of war-torn cities.

CONVERSIONS

- **PzKfw III (Flamm) Ausf. M (Sd. Kfz 141/3)** - flame-thrower
- **Befehlswagen III Ausf. Dl (Sd. Kfz 267-268)** - command tank
- **Befehlswagen III Ausf. E (Sd. Kfz 267-268)** - command tank
- **Befehlswagen III Ausf. H (Sd. Kfz 266-268)** - command tank
- **Befehlswagen III Ausf. K** - command tank
- **Beobachtungswagen III** - observation vehicle (Sd. Kfz 143)

The early version of the Panzer III was equipped with a 37mm main gun. Even before they saw combat these guns were already known to be unsuitable for most tanks.

Armour (mm/angle) Ausf H	Armour (mm/angle) Ausf L/M
Front Turret: 30/13	Front Turret: 57/15
Front Upper Hull: 30+30/90	Front Upper Hull: 50+20/9
Front Lower Hull: 30+30/23	Front Lower Hull: 50/21
Side Turret: 30/25	Side Turret: 30/25
Side Upper Hull: 30/0	Side Upper Hull: 30/0
Side Lower Hull: 30/0	Side Lower Hull: 30/0
Rear Turret: 30/13	Rear Turret: 30/12
Rear Upper Hull: 30/30	Rear Upper Hull: 50/17
Rear Lower Hull: 30+30/8	Rear Lower Hull: 50/9
Turret Top/ Bottom: 10/89	Turret Top / Bottom: 10/83
Upper Hull Top / Bottom: 17/77	Upper Hull Top / Bottom: 18/79
Lower Hull Top / Bottom: 16/90	Lower Hull Tip / Bottom: 16/90
Gun Mantlet: 37/0	Gun Mantlet: 50+20/0

Model	Ausf H	Ausf L/M
Weight	21800 kg	22700 kg
Crew	5	5
Engine	Maybach HL 120 TRM 12-cylinder / 265 hp	Maybach HL 120 TRM 12-cylinder / 265 hp
Speed	Road: 40 km/h Crosscountry: 20 km/h	Road: 40 km/h Crosscountry: 20 km/h
Range	Road: 165 km Crosscountry: 105 km	Road: 155 km Crosscountry: 95 km
Fuel Capacity	320 litres	320 litres
Length	5.52 m (with the gun)	6.41 m (with the gun) 5.56 m (with the gun)
Width	2.95 m	2.95 m
Height	2.50 m	2.50 m
Armament	50 mm KwK 38 L/42 2 x 7.92 mm MG34 (1 x MG - hull) (1 x MG - coax)	50 mm KwK 38 L/60 2 x 7.92 mm MG34 (1 x MG - hull) (1 x MG - coax)
Ammunition Supply	50 mm - 99 rounds 7.92 mm - 2700 rounds	50 mm - 92 rounds 7.92 mm - 3750 rounds

Raw materials used in the production of the Pz. Kpfw III	
Steel	39000 kg
Tin	1.40 kg
Copper	60.10 kg
Aluminium	90.40 kg
Lead	71.10 kg
Zinc	49.10 kg
Rubber	125 kg

The Panzer Mark III was a highly reliable machine mechanically but was undergunned and was phased out in 1942.

INTO BATTLE

"Teamwork between the Panzers and the infantry was exemplary. They quickly began to work together without apparent difficulty. The place of the armour leader is at the head of the formation. He can only command his unit properly from the front"

AFTER ACTION REPORT, POLAND 1939

The first moves in Hitler's master plan had been achieved without bloodshed, but as tensions rose, Adolf Hitler's crooked path led only downwards into chaos. The conquest of Poland heralded the coming of the Second World War.

On Friday, 1 September 1939, the tactical principles of the Panzerwaffe still had to be put to the test. The German attack began at 4:45 am, when the Battleship Schleswig-Holstein on a so-culled 'goodwill visit' opened fire on a Polish naval depot and garrison at Westeplatte. An hour later the first German units crossed the border. On 3 September 1939 Great Britain and France declared war on Germany.

Originally, Germany was to invade Poland in the early hours of 26th August 1939, but at 8:00pm on 25th August, Hitler postponed the attack. The final order was transmitted at 4:00pm on 31st August, but was only given to the troops at 4:45am on 1 September 1939. The invasion was preceded by numerous German border provocations and diversions including the notorious incident at the radio station at Gliwice staged by German troops in Polish uniforms.

Hitler was about to plunge Europe into years of barbarity and turmoil on an unprecedented scale. Although the Polish campaign was predominantly a conventional war, the German battle plan did include some elements of what was to become known as 'Blitzkrieg'. Hitler made no declaration of war for example, a fact which, unbelievably, caught his victims off guard every time it occurred during the war and which gave him the vital advantage of surprise.

Attacks by the Luftwaffe preceded the invasion. Screaming over Poland ahead of the main

A war artist provides a vivid impression of the co-operation between the Panzer Grenadiers and the tanks in action in Russia during 1942.

armies their task was to destroy the Polish air force and then to act as airborne artillery for the ground forces. Spreading terror among the civilians was also an important part of their mission. The attempt to destroy the Polish air force on the ground was only partially successful, since many of their warplanes were moved to new locations. Nonetheless, air superiority was quickly established, and by day three the Polish air force had been virtually annihilated.

From the start, the Germans engaged in an innovative new form of mobile warfare. At vital stages during the attacks, Stukas hurtled earthwards to place their bombs almost to within centimetres of the centre of their targets. Co-ordination between the air force, the motorised and armoured formations was exemplary, providing enormous flexibility, especially in the absence of artillery support.

THE GERMAN FORCES

The German invading force was divided into five armies and reserves, all under command of General Walther von Brauchitsch. The Germans attacked from three directions – Silesia/Moravia and Slovakia, Western Pomerania and East Prussia. Colonel General Gerd von Rundstedt's Army Group South, which was composed of the 8th, 10th and 14th Armies, attacked from Silesia/ Moravia and Slovakia and had the strongest complement of armoured formations, with over 2000 tanks and 800 armoured cars in four Panzer Divisions, four Light Divisions and two Motorised Divisions.

General Gunther von Kluge's 4th Army, part of Colonel General Fedor von Bock's Army Group North, attacked from Western Pomerania, with eight Infantry Divisions, two Motorised Divisions and one Panzer Division. General George von Kuechler's 3rd Army, also part of Army Group North, attacked from East Prussia with two Infantry Divisions and one Panzer Division. Altogether Army Group North boasted 600 tanks and 200 armoured cars. All three attacks were designed to converge on Warsaw. In total, German forces included 1,850,000 infantry, supported by over 3,000 tanks and 10,000 artillery pieces. The Luftwaffe deployed 2,085 aeroplanes grouped in two air fleets. Additionally the attacking force held advantage by being able to attack Poland from three directions at once. The Germans also had a well-established spy network and could count on the help of many ethnic Germans living in Poland; the Germans also knew the Polish rail and road network very well as German firms had built it.

Units of the Panzerwaffe were equipped with four types of tanks: 1445 PzKpfw I, 1226

Panzer IIIs and IVs of the 14th Panzer Division move through a Russian village in the months prior to the attack on Stalingrad.

PzKpfw II light tanks and around 100 PzKpfw III and 211 Pzkpfw IV medium tanks. In addition, there were 215 command tanks and other armoured vehicles including the Czech PzKpfw 35(t) and a few 38(t). Each of the Panzer Divisions fielded around 300 tanks. Along with the tanks, there were some 308 heavy armoured cars and 718 light armoured cars; the few lucky Panzer Grenadiers were transported in one of 68 armoured personnel carriers.

The Polish Army fielded 39 Infantry, 11 Elite Cavalry Brigades, three Mountain Brigades and two Armoured Motorised Brigades along with various support units. The Army Groups, 'Lodz', 'Krakow' and 'Karpaty' between them had 241 tanks and 32 armoured cars. Army groups 'Pomorze', 'Poznan' and 'Modlin' deployed some 234 tanks and 52 armoured cars. The Reserve formations had some 185 tanks between them. The Polish Army was not yet fully mobilised or prepared for war, as according to the Polish defence plan - Z. Nonetheless, the Poles responded to German attacks on all fronts, attempting to contain the invading force in order to counter-attack. Polish planners correctly predicted directions of German attacks but knew that they could only delay them in order to allow their Allies time to act. In total, the Polish forces fielded some one million infantry, approximately 900 tanks and 4,300 artillery pieces supported by 400 aeroplanes. Only a small percentage of all Polish equipment was modern, the rest largely obsolete, as Poland had only begun the process of reorganisation and modernisation in 1936. The Polish army lacked motorised transport and relied on infantry and horse-drawn transport. In addition the Polish army was surrounded by the enemy on three sides along a 3,000-kilometre-long frontier.

On September 1st and 2nd, the Polish forces were already involved in heavy fighting in the Battles of Mlawa, in Pomerania, while retreating eastwards in attempt to establish a line of defence and delay the invaders. Polish forces made up of infantry on foot were unable to fall hack and establish defensive lines as they were constantly pursued and outpaced by German motorised and Panzer units. Many Polish units and even armies were surrounded and destroyed, while attempting to either defend or withdraw. The Polish High Command realised as early as 5 September that the situation was critical and there was no hope without immediate assistance from its Allies. Many units were cut off but continued fighting. After heavy fighting and desperate defence, on 8 September the Germans reached Warsaw.

On 9th September the bloodiest and most bitter battle of the entire campaign began. The Battle of Bzura was a Polish counteroffensive designed to relieve Warsaw. It was executed by Army Groups 'Pomorze' and 'Poznan', both of which were in danger of being surrounded themselves. At first the Poles were successful and inflicted heavy losses on the German forces principally due to the element of surprise. Again, the speed of the German units made further operations impossible and by 16th September Germans began pushing the Polish Army towards Warsaw.

When Hitler visited the tank corps soon after the invasion, it was the destruction that the Panzer divisions had caused which astonished him most. The Blitzkrieg elements were falling smoothly into place.

Although brilliantly conceived and executed, the overall German strategy was still based on the classic German tradition of encirclement and envelopment carried out mainly by conventional forces.

By September Poland's situation was already beyond hope. Despite the obvious hopelessness of the situation, on 18th September the largest tank-versus-tank engagement of the campaign took place near Tomaszow Lubelski. The battle ended on 20th September with the total destruction of Polish forces under General Tadeusz Kutrzeba. Although it delayed the capitulation of Warsaw, the battle fought in a lost cause.

The first German attack on Warsaw took place on 9th September, but from then until 24 September Polish defenders successfully resisted all attacks. On 25th September the Germans began a ground and aerial bombardment of the city, and from 25th-27th September unsuccessfully attempted to storm the city. Many tanks were lost in the street fighting, which again underlined the flaws in the Panzer I. On 28th September, Warsaw capitulated because of the extreme conditions and lack of supplies. At the same time, from 10th September, Fortress Modlin (under General Wiktor Thommee) was also unsuccessfully attacked by the Germans, until its capitulation on 29th September.

A Pz.Kpfw (35)t lies abandoned in a tank graveyard. This particular example has been gutted by fire and has lost its turret-mounted machine gun. This Czech-made tank provided an important stop-gap during the early campaigns.

Stalin had been unpleasantly surprised by the speed of the German advance. Even with the supposed security of a non-aggression pact with Hitler in his pocket, Stalin did not want to see Germany control the whole of Poland.

On Sunday 17th September the Red Army invaded Poland from the east to 'liberate' and 'protect' Belorussians and Ukrainians living in Eastern Poland. This came as a shock to the Poles and made regrouping of remaining Polish forces an impossible task. The Soviet invasion force was made up of two fronts - Timoszenko's Ukrainian and Kowalow's Belorussian. Both fronts consisted of 1.5 million soldiers, 6,191 tanks, 1,800 aeroplanes and 9,140 artillery pieces. After heavy fighting, on 18th September, the Soviets captured Wilno, followed by Grodno and Lwow on 22nd September, reaching River Bug on 23rd September.

On the night of 18th September the Polish President and High Command along with a single armoured battalion equipped with French Renault R-35 tanks entered Romania, where they were interned. On 18th September Germans and Soviets met in Bresc and Bugiem and exchanged 'greetings'. On 2nd October Polish defenders of Hel (under Rear Admiral Unrug) capitulated. The last battle of the Polish campaign took place on 2nd-5th October - the Battle of Kock. On Friday, 6th October 1939 the last Polish troops capitulated.

The Polish Army of 1939 used a variety of vehicles. Those included: 574 TK and TKS tankettes (light reconnaissance tanks), 102 obsolete Renault FT-17 light tanks, 160 7TP light tanks and 50 British Vickers 6-ton tanks, along with approximately one hundred armoured cars.

The Polish Army's tanks were grouped in light tank battalions and light tank companies, but they were scattered throughout the army. Tankettes served with the infantry divisions, cavalry brigades and independent units attached to larger units. In addition, Poland had a single Mechanised Brigade. The Polish light tanks and tankettes were the first opponents for the German Panzers. Patriotic but outnumbered Polish tank crews with their mostly outclassed equipment fought bravely and managed to destroy a number of German vehicles, as they simultaneously defended their homeland from both the Germans and the Soviets. The Polish Campaign is surrounded by numerous myths such as the destruction of The Polish airforce in the opening hours of the invasion and vain cavalry charges against German armoured units. Both stories were creations of German and some Italian propaganda, and are very far from the truth. The Polish airforce was deployed at numerous airfields and, although numerically inferior and partially obsolete, was very active during the course of the campaign up to and including the battle for Warsaw. Polish cavalry brigades never charged tanks with their sabres or lances. They were conventionally equipped with weapons such as 37mm Bofors wz.36 (model 1936) anti-tank guns. At the time of the battles the cavalry brigades were in the process of being reorganised into motorised brigades so the men in the ranks were well aware of the realities of modem warfare.

THE COST OF VICTORY

German casualties in the campaign amounted to around 10,000 killed and 30,000 wounded. Although significant, those losses were very low compared to Polish casualties of which 66,000 were killed, 133,000 wounded and 420,000 taken prisoner. In addition, the Germans had 1,000 armoured fighting vehicles knocked out during the campaign, mainly disabled by anti-tank guns. According to German sources only 89 PzKpfw I, 83 PzKpfw II, 26 PzKpfw III, 19 PzKpfw IV, 7 PzKpfw 35(t) and 7 Pzkpfw 38(t) were complete write-offs. That aside, it should be noted that the Polish campaign proved to be the most costly and challenging campaign for the Germans, until the invasion of the Soviet Union in June of 1941.

Some 70,000 Polish soldiers escaped to Hungary and Romania, 20,000 to Latvia and Lithuania, the majority eventually making their way west to continue fighting. On 30th September the Polish Government in Exile was established in Paris.

WITTMANN IN BATTLE

In the ranks of the Leibstandarte Adolf Hitler was the fledgling tank ace Michael Wittmann. The Leibstandarte Motorised Regiment fought hard in Poland from the first day of the campaign. On that day the armoured scout platoon was soon in action, and Wittmann had received his baptism of fire. The campaign in Poland was brief (only 30 days in duration) but, nonetheless, his experiences had whetted his appetite for combat. In the following year Wittmann and his armoured car again saw action in the rapid campaign that led to the fall of France.

The Polish campaign demonstrated the speed and power possessed by Panzers and the excellence of the Panzer Divisions. It also demonstrated that the time of large armies made up of infantry marching on foot and cavalry was over. At the same time, it provided the Germans with real experience of using armour in combat conditions.

Above all the Germans learned that tanks were not suited for combat in built up areas: heavy losses had been suffered in the direct assault on Warsaw. They also discovered that well organised anti-tank defences are very costly for tank forces to assault in the absence of proper preparation.

A war artist's impression of German tanks moving through a burning Russian village published in the April 1942 edition of Signal, the propaganda magazine.

What the Polish Campaign also proved beyond doubt was that PzKpfw I and II were unsuitable to be used as front-line combat tanks and should be completely replaced with the heavier PzKpfw III and IV. The other sobering lesson was that during the course of the campaign the Light Divisions had proved to be unsuccessful, being too weak to perform the tasks of either Cavalry or motorised infantry.

THE DANGEROUS WORLD

The tank was the catalyst for success and gave the Nazi regime a stunning propaganda coup. The reality of battle, however, had been a sobering experience for many crews. In tank-versus-tank contests the crews prayed that their first shot would hit, turning the enemy vehicle into a flaming mass, as the fuel and ammunition exploded. A miss could mean their own destruction by return.

The prospect of the awful death of men trapped in a burning tank haunted the tank crews. In the footage from all of the major tank battles of the Second World War, from Poland through North Africa, and into Russia, the black columns of smoke from burning vehicles can be seen hanging on the horizon like gathering storm clouds. All too often they marked the Funeral pyres for their hapless crews.

Death or injury could come to the tank crews from a myriad of sources. It was not always necessary to even damage the vehicle. One other ever-present danger for tank crews were metal splinters caused by direct hits on the outside of a tank. As the outside velocity of the impact converted into violent internal energy, these deadly fragments were blown from the inside of the turret, where they would fly around the inside of the tank slicing through the bodies of the crewmen packed together in their claustrophobic world. Riveted tanks in particular were most susceptible to this unpleasant phenomenon, which made the 35(t) and 38(t) deeply unpopular with the crews.

CAPTURED POLISH ARMOUR

On a more positive note, the Polish Campaign provided Germans with a supply of captured Polish armoured fighting vehicles, including the 7TP three-man light tank and the TK series of two-man tankettes for light reconnaissance. These were locally produced versions of the British Vickers tanks and tankettes. The 7TP light tank was the Polish army's main battle tank and some 170 were in service as of September 1939.

On 11th September 1939 Adolf Hitler's order stated that military equipment was to he collected from the battlefields and moved to special collection points. Captured 7TPs were designated as Panzerkampfwagen 7TP 731(p), while TK-3s were designated as Leichte Panzerkampfwagen TK(p), TKS as Leichte Panzerkampfwagen TKS(p) and C2P as Artillerie Schlepper C2P(p).

During the course of the campaign the 5th Panzer Division had actually pressed captured TK series tankettes into service, while the 1st Panzer Division also used a few captured 7TP tanks. The 1st Panzer Regiment's 4th Company's commander, Second Lieutenant Fritz Kraemer, is known to have used one of them after his own machine was disabled. It remained in the original Polish camouflage scheme hastily painted with white crosses on the sides of the turret along with the number '400' representing command tank of 4th Company.

On 5th October 1939 a grand Victory Parade took place in Warsaw and a small number (probably eighteen) captured 7TPs now belonging to the 203rd Panzer Abteilung stationed in Spala were presented to Adolf Hitler. A single captured 7TP, with its frontal armour plate penetrated by a 20mm anti-tank projectile, was displayed during the Leipzig International Fair in March 1940.

Following the Polish campaign, captured tankettes were repaired in the workshops in Warsaw and then pressed into service by Wehrmacht units stationed in the General Government of Poland. In 1940 two platoons of TKS tankettes were certainly part of a light Panzer company. In

Warsaw a number of captured 7TPs were used as headquarters tanks in 1939/40, probably with 203rd Panzer Abteilung. In 1940 this unit was moved to Norway and later to France. A number of 7TPs anil TKS tankettes took part in the 1st anniversary of the General Government parade in Warsaw on 6th October 1940. Afterwards 7TPs were used for internal policing duties and later on as artillery tractors.

In Germany there was jubilation and a sense of restored national pride. The nation's virile leader acquired new prestige and laurels from the fatherland, and the Third Reich felt that it was entering into a glorious new world of its own making.

A command version of the Panzer I photographed in August 1941. These vehicles were clearly redundant at the time of the Spanish Civil War. Only Hitler's brinkmanship forced an unwelcome and unexpected war on the Panzerwaffe which meant that these unsuitable machines would see action in the Russian campaign.

PANZERKAMPFWAGEN IV SD.KFZ.161

Originally designed as an infantry support tank with a unique tactical role. Although the Panzer IV had thin armour, it carried a powerful 75mm gun and could match any other tank at that time. The prototype of the Panzer IV was given the code name Bataillonfuhrerwagen. The Panzer IV was ordered by Hitler from Krupp, MAN and Rheinmetall Borsig to weigh in at 18 tonnes with a top speed of 35 km/hr. The Krupp design - the VK 200 1 (K) - was eventually selected to enter into full-scale production in 1935. Along with the Panther, it was to become the main combat tank of the Third Reich.

The PzKpfw IV was perceived as the 'workhorse' of all the Panzer divisions and more were produced than any other variant in the 1933-1945 period. The Ausf A was built as a pre-production vehicle and only 35 were produced. The modifications from this gave rise to the Ausf B which emerged in 1938 with an increased frontal armour thickness and a six-speed gearbox, which enhanced its cross-country performance. That same year Krupp-Gruson produced the Ausf C and 134 of this model were in production until 1939.

The Ausf D/E saw an upgrading of its armour thickness and improved vision blocks for the driver. The Ausf E was the first of the Panzer IV fitted with turret mounted stowage bins. The Ausf F 1, produced between 1941-1942 was the last Panzer IV to be based on the short version chassis. 25 of the F Is were converted into Ausf F2s (it had the British nickname of "Mark IV Special" because it was far superior to any other tank at the time). It was followed by the modified version of the Ausf G in May 1942.

The Ausf H, introduced in April 1943, was exclusively armed with a newer version of the 75mm KwK 40 L/48 gun and was fitted with steel/wire armour skirts. Over 3,770 of

Panzer IV Ausf. C

PzKpfw IV Ausf. D

the P/zKpfw IV Ausf H were made and saw action. Even in 1945 the last model, the Ausf J, was an effective weapon given the right crew. A selected number of the Ausf H and J were also converted into command tanks or observation tanks towards the end of the war period.

To its ultimate credit, the PzKpfw IV was the only German tank to stay in production throughout all the war hostilities. It was spacious inside and preferred by crews over the Panther, Tiger and King Tiger as it was more technically reliable.

Armour (mm/angle) Ausf D	Armour (mm/angle) Ausf G
Front Turret: 30/10	Front Turret: 50/11
Front Upper Hull: 30/7	Front Upper Hull: 50 or 50+30/10
Front Lower Hull: 30/12	Front Lower Hull: 50 or 50+30/12
Side Turret: 20/25	Side Turret: 30/26
Side Upper Hull: 20/0	Side Upper Hull: 30/0
Side Lower Hull: 20/0	Side Lower Hull: 30/0
Rear Turret: 20/0	Rear Turret: 30/10
Rear Upper Hull: 20/9	Rear Upper Hull: 20/12
Rear Lower Hull: 20/10	Rear Lower Hull: 20/9
Turret Top/ Bottom: 10/83	Turret Top / Bottom: 10/83
Upper Hull Top / Bottom: 12/84	Upper Hull Top / Bottom: 12/85
Lower Hull Top / Bottom: 10/90	Lower Hull Tip / Bottom: 10/90
Gun Mantlet: 35/0	Gun Mantlet: 50/0

Model	Ausf A	Ausf B	Ausf C/D	Ausf E	Ausf F1	Ausf F2/G	Ausf H/J
Weight	17.3 tonnes	17.7 tonnes	20 tonnes	21 tonnes	22.3 tonnes	23.6 tonnes	25 tonnes
Crew	5	5	5	5	5	5	5
Engine	Maybach HL 108 TR V-12 250 BHP	Maybach HL 120 TRM V-12 300 BHP	Maybach HL 120 TRM V-12 300 BHP	Maybach HL 120 TRM V-12 300 BHP	Maybach HL 120 TRM V-12 300 BHP	Maybach HL 120 TRM V-12 300 BHP	Maybach HL 120 TRM V-12 300 BHP
Speed	32 km/h	40 km/h	40 km/h	40 km/h	40 km/h	40 km/h	40 km/h
Range (Road)	250 km	260 km	230 km	220 km	200 km	190 km	Ausf H - 180 km Ausf J - 270 km
Fuel Capacity	443 litres	470 litres	470 litres	470 litres	470 litres	470 litres	Ausf H - 470 litres Ausf J - 680 litres
Length	5.60 m	5.87 m	Ausf C - 5.87 m Ausf D - 5.92 m	5.92 m	5.93 m	6.63 m	6.63 m
Width	2.75 m	2.75 m	Ausf C - 2.75 m Ausf D - 2.86 m	2.86 m	2.88 m	2.88 m	2.88 m
Height	2.65 m	2.65 m	Ausf C - 2.65 m Ausf D - 2.68 m	2.68 m	2.68 m	2.68 m	2.68 m
Armament	L/24 & 2 x 7.92 mm MG	L/24 & 1 x 7.92 mm MG	L/24 & 1 x 7.92 mm MG	L/24 & 1 x 7.92 mm MG	L/24 & 1 x 7.92 mm MG	L/24 & 1 x 7.92 mm MG	L/24 & 1 x 7.92 mm MG

CONVERSIONS

FLAKPANZERS (AIR DEFENCE)
- **Mobelwagen** - Sd.Kfz. 161/3
- **Wirbelwind**
- **Ostwind**

PANZERJÄGERS / STURMPANZERS
(TANK DESTROYERS AND ASSAULT GUNS)
- **Hornisse / Nashorn** - Sd.Kfz. 164
- **Hummel** - Sd.Kfz. 165
- **Panzerjäger IV** - Sd.Kfz. 162 162/1
- **Sturmgeschütz** - Sd.Kfz. 163 / 167
- **Sturmpanzer IV Brummbar** - Sd.Kfz. 166

PROTOTYPES / PROJECTS
- **Geschutzwagen IV (Sd. Kfz. 165/1)** - 105 mm L/28 howitzer carrier
- **Geschutzwagen IV (Sd. Kfz. 165/1)** - 75 mm Pak 39 L/48 gun carrier
- **Geschutzwagen IV (Sd. Kfz. 165/1)** - 105 mm L/28 howitzer carrier - (Rh) prototype
- **Heuschrecke 10 / Gw IVb** - 105 mm L/28 - 3 prototypes built
- **Panzerjäger 105** - 105 mm K18 L/52 gun - 2 prototypes built
- **Panzerkampwagen IV mit hydrostatischen Antrieb**
- **Ostwind II**
- **Zerstorer 45**
- **Kugelblitz**
- **Panzer IV with 2 x 75 mm rifles and 20/30 mm target gun** (planned)
- **Pz. Kpfw. IV Ausf C/D/E mounted with rocket projectors** (experimental)
- **Pz. Kpfw. IV Ausf F2/H mit 75 mm Kwk. 42 L/70** (experimental)
- **Pz. Kpfw. IV Ausf D mit 50 mm Kwk. 39 L/60** (experimental)
- **Pz. Kpfw. IV Ausf H with Schmallturm turret** (project)
- **Sturmpanzer IV** - 305 mm Morser M 16 carrier (planned)
- **Pz. Kpfw. IV Ausf C mit Minenrollen** - Pz. Kpfw. IV with mine roller

OTHER
- **Befehlswagen IV Ausf H/J** - command tank
- **Beobachtungswagen IV Ausf J** - observation vehicle
- **Munitionspanzerwagen IV** - ammunition carrier
- **Panzer IV Ausf D (75 mm L/24 gun)** - submersible tank
- **Bruckenleger IV** - bridging vehicle Ausf C/D
- **Infanterie Sturmsteg auf Pz. KPfw. IV** - assault bridge
- **Panzerfahre** - amphibious armoured ferry
- **Munitionsschlepper fur Karlgerat - Ausf D/F** - ammunition carrier
- **Bergepanzer IV** - recovery vehicle

HITLER TURNS WEST

"The confident feelings among the Panzertruppen are based chiefly upon our superior combat elan and only secondly on our fire power. The total of gun armed Panzers is less than those allocated to the French Forces. Improvement is necessary in these areas."

OBERST KUEHN, 3RD PANZER BRIGADE, JUNE 6 1940

Among Germany's enemies dismay and apprehension reigned. Their disquiet was well founded. The next display of German military expertise, code-named 'Exercise Weser', was to be equally ruthless. Norway and Denmark were both neutral countries. Their strategic importance became crystal clear, however, when Hitler realised that Germany's supplies of iron ore from Sweden could easily be severed by an allied invasion. On 7th April German forces launched their invasion of Denmark and Norway by land, sea and air, to grant those countries the euphemistically phrased 'Protection of the Third Reich'. The Wehrmacht swept over the border into Denmark, and as troops landed at Copenhagen the Luftwaffe circled ominously overhead. Denmark had no choice but to accept an ultimatum and surrendered early on 9th April to its mighty neighbour. Norway had last seen a war in 1814 and was totally unprepared for the invasion.

Destroyers protected by the Scharnhorst and the Gneisenau transported mountain troops to Trondheim and Narvik, where they were landed by amphibious craft, and similar landings took place at Oslo, Kristiansand and Bergen. Once again the speed of German activity had rendered the plans of her enemies ineffective. Three of the experimental heavy tanks, Neubau-Panzerkampfwagen IV, were deployed during the short campaign in Norway, but although they did see some action, the real purpose was the propaganda value. This was to be the one and only

Grenadiers advance past a knocked-out allied tank. The unpopular riveted construction of many of the early war tanks can clearly be seen in this example.

deployment of the Neubau-Panzerkampfwagen IV in action. From now on only the Panzer IV would be deployed in the infantry support role.

The door to Scandinavia was now slammed in Britain's face and, buoyed with success, the Führer confidently focused on a more glorious prize than any he had yet attained - France.

France was Germany's ancient enemy and had been her humiliator at Versailles. Hitler initiated planning for 'Fall Gelb' - Case Yellow.

Case Yellow was repeatedly postponed. The delay was put to good use, as an intensive study of the Polish campaign was undertaken. The role of the armoured divisions and the other Blitzkrieg components came under particular scrutiny. One of the men eager to discover what improvements could be introduced was Heinz Guderian.

Since the Great War Guderian had worked extensively with wireless, and gained invaluable experience in the deployment of infantry, artillery and aircraft. He had a clear vision of the force he wished to create. He had won the battle to ensure that his tanks would be concentrated in armoured divisions, not dispersed in small numbers. They would be spearheads of a single, large military formation, also encompassing aircraft, artillery and mechanised infantry. The commander would not be stationed far in the rear, but would operate near the front, responding instantly to changing situations and issuing orders by wireless directly to his units.

Making the most efficient use possible of available technology was only part of Guderian's work. He also had a clear understanding of the value of proper training, and knew that it was vital to encourage drive and initiative even in the lowest ranks. The German army as a whole had incomparable standards: the men of the tank arm were trained to an even higher pitch.

By the early months of 1940 Guderian was moving steadily closer to realising his ideal of a highly mobile, integrated striking force. In Poland the tanks had rarely driven more than ten miles a day. Now Guderian disposed of larger, far more modem forces, to be used in the first full-scale experiment in Blitzkrieg tactics. Early in the morning of 10th May 1940 Fall Gelb was activated. German forces swung down into the Low Countries and the term 'Blitzkrieg' a synonym for terror and death, was burned into the pages of history.

As the tide of Hitler's conquests now turned to the west the Germans would be fighting more modern armies equipped with at least equal and sometimes superior equipment. The British and French forces also had superiority in numbers and were much better prepared than the Poles. By a combination of careful planning, surprise and some very daring innovations, the Germans were able to make the victory against Poland seem like a side-show. New tactics, such as the German Paratroopers who were dropped on top of the major Belgian fortification of Even Emael in gliders, made their first appearance on the modern battlefield during this campaign. The Maginot Line that stretched along the majority of the French border to the east was easily bypassed when German Panzers advanced through Ardennes region in Belgium. Once past here they advanced all the way to the coast with little in their way to stop them. What had proved impossible in four years of trench warfare during the First World War was to be accomplished in the space of six weeks. In France the value of the tank in modern warfare would be well and truly established.

THE BRITISH TANKS

Without the restrictions which had been placed on Germany, the main allied countries of Britain and France had also been engaged in developing their weapons during the '20s and '30s. They did, however, take different routes. The other major nations had not always recognised the full potential of the tank and therefore design and innovation in this aspect were rather more limited. France had relegated the tank to the role of an infantry support weapon. Britain had seen the potential of this new machine and set about developing new designs. By the outbreak of the Second World War they had come up with four main designs.

The Matilda Mk I was designated a light tank and weighed 11 tons. It was crewed by two men. The main armament was provided by a Vickers machine gun. Like the Panzer I this tank was little more than an armoured machine gun carrier. However, unlike the Panzer I, this vehicle had very

A French tank man surrenders to German grenadiers. Although better armed and armoured than the German machines, the French tank forces were hampered by inferior organisation and tactics.

good armour protection 60mm thick. This was double the thickness of the best German tank at the time. For a light tank it had a very low top speed of 8mph. The Matilda I's limitations were cruelly exposed in the French campaign. Although it protected its crew well, it was no match for the determined German Panzer crews. The one-man turret was also a major drawback. Over one hundred and forty of these machines were sent to France, but all of them were lost in that campaign.

The Cruiser Mk IV was an improved design that weighed in slightly heavier at 15 tons. It had a four-man crew that allowed for better results in battle. The main armament was the two-pound gun backed up with a Vickers machine gun. The armour was not as thick as the Matilda 1, but was still good at 38mm. The top speed of this tank was 30mph. It had excellent suspension but the engine suffered from reliability problems. Over three hundred of them saw action in the French campaign.

The A9 Mk I Cruiser weighed in at 13 tons and was crewed by six men. The main firepower was the two-pounder gun, but this time it was backed up with three Vickers machine guns. It was thinly armoured at 14mm but had a good top speed of 25mph. Like the Cruiser Mk IV, the structural design consisted of many angles that trapped the armour-piercing enemy shells This, coupled with the thin armour, resulted in many of them being lost in the French campaign.

The best of the British machines, the Matilda II, was an infantry support tank. The Matilda II weighed 27 tons and had a crew of four. It was armed with a two-pounder gun backed up with a Vickers machine gun. It was very well protected with 78mm thick armour. The speed was a maximum 15mph. This tank performed reasonably well and remained in service after the fall of France.

THE FRENCH TANKS

French thinking in tank use was influential in the design of their new machines. Like the British, they had four main designs available at the start of the French campaign.

The Char Somua S-35 was a medium tank weighing 20 tons, manned by a crew of three. A 47mm main gun, backed up with a 7.5mm machine gun, provided the armament. The armour protection was very good, at 55mm. It had a top speed of 25mph. This tank was more than capable of tackling the Panzers of 1940 vintage and was well designed. This was one of the few captured French tanks which the Germans made use of in the army after the campaign was over.

The Char B 1 was the heaviest tank in use by the French, weighing 32 tons. It was manned by a crew of four, which was too few. The main firepower consisted of one 75mm gun, situated in the hull. This was backed up by a 47mm gun located in the turret. In addition there were two 7.5mm machine guns-on board. The armour protection was an excellent 60mm but the speed was limited to 17mph. Despite the glaring flaws, this tank was to give a good account of itself in the fight against the Germans. The Germans found that this beast could be easily knocked out by a well-placed shell in the ventilation grill. At the start of the French campaign this was probably the most formidable tank in use.

Also facing the powerful forces was the Hotchkiss H.35 - one of the two light tanks in use by the French. It weighed in at 12 tons and had a two-man crew. The weapons that were fitted to this tank were a 37mm main gun backed up with a 7.5mm machine gun. The armour on this tank was a very respectable 40mm, and the top speed was also good at 22mph.

The Renault R35 was another one of the French light tanks. It weighed 10 tons and was manned by a crew of two. It also had a 37mm main gun backed up with one 7.5mm machine gun. The armour protection was 45mm thick. However, top speed was only 12mph.

On balance, the allied machines, and in particular the French tanks, outclassed the Germans in armour protection and main armament. The Germans were surprised to find that their 37mm anti-tank gun was ineffective against the thick armour of these tanks. The downfall of the allied tanks was the way in which they were employed tactically and also some of their design faults, like the one-man turrets used in the French machines.

CASE YELLOW

The invasion of France was code-named 'Case Yellow'. The plan had been devised by von Manstein, but had been credited to Hitler. It was a variation of the Schlieffen Plan from the First World War. The Schlieffen plan had the objective of drawing the allies into the Low Countries. They would follow this by swinging through behind the allies and ending up in Paris, thereby encircling the allied forces. The plan had just failed in the First World War, but the Germans were confident that it would bring them victory this time. However, the plans for Operation Yellow had fallen into the hands of the allies through an unfortunate accident. This meant that the German staff had to rethink their plan of attack. This time von Manstein envisaged a spoiling attack in the Low Countries, like the original plan. The main change was the direction of the main thrust. It would be delivered through the Ardennes region which was thought to be tank-proof. For the attack the Germans split their forces into three Army Groups. Army Group B would advance through Holland and Belgium, thereby providing the bait for the allies. Army Group A would move through the Ardennes and would provide the main thrust. Army Group C would be opposite the Maginot Line and would keep the French defenders busy. The main thrust had the objective of racing through the enemy positions and on towards the French coast near Bolougne and Calais.

The allies anticipated a re-run of the First World War plan and they distributed their forces accordingly. The bulk of them were positioned north in readiness for the expected attack through the Low Countries. They had two further lines of reserves: one of these was positioned in the Ardennes region. The allies grossly overestimated the tank strength of the Germans and thought that they had over seven thousand tanks.

The reality was that, although the Panzerwaffe had now been expanded to ten Panzer Divisions, the Germans had just over 2,400 tanks for the attack. In the form of the Panzer I, over 1,400 of these were no more than armoured machine gun carriers. The allies had over 3,300 tanks to field against the Germans. In the important areas of main gun and armour protection, the allied machines outclassed the German tanks.

When the attack began in the early hours of 10th May it caught the allies by surprise. The Germans made quick gains and good advances. This was helped considerably as the allied strength was in the north, whereas the bulk of the German strength would smash through the Ardennes, further south. The allied thinking had lulled them into a false sense of security and they felt confident that they would destroy the Germans easily. Although the Germans lacked numerical superiority in machines, they had been training hard on their new concepts and had tested the co-ordination of their forces. The concept was fairly simple, but very effective and advanced for the time.

A point of impact would be chosen that was small in width. The armour would concentrate on this central point and the weight of firepower would be used to overwhelm the enemy. Once a breech had been made the rest of the Division would rush through the gap and into the rear enemy areas. The tanks would continue to race deep inside the enemy lines, whilst the infantry and artillery would deal with any pockets of resistance and capture key objectives. The anti-tank gunners would set up a defensive screen to protect the areas already captured. Under this well coordinated attack, the allies fell back in confusion and panic. They were still thinking of the last war and were prepared for a defensive battle. The Germans had proved that a rapid deep advance into the enemy lines provided its own defence.

PANZERKAMPFWAGEN 35(T)

Between the wars the new Czech nation maintained an advanced defence industry with a production capability extending to light and medium tanks. In 1935/36, Skoda's LT(Light Tank) vz.(model) 35 entered service. It was designed to rival a range of foreign vehicles in service at the time such as the Polish 7TP, the British Vickers 6 ton, the Soviet T-26, the Italian Carro Armato M 11139 and M13/40 and the German PzKpfw III tanks. The LT-35 equipped four fast divisions of the Czech Army as of 1938. During its service with the Czech Army, the LT-35 gained a reputation as an unreliable vehicle and it was only considered to be a "interim solution" before the LT-38, (later PzKpfw 38(t)) could be fully developed and ready for production. The LT-35's unreliable reputation was due to its untested but advanced technical design. By 1938 most of its teething problems were solved and overall the LT-35 proved to be a reasonably good tank. LT-35s were produced in different variants and were also known under different designations such as R-2 and T-I1. Before the war the LT-35 was also sold to other countries including Bulgaria and Romania. The 1938/39 German take-over of the Czechoslovak state meant that in March of 1939 219 LT-35s were confiscated from the Czech Army and most were incorporated into the German Army. A small number remained in service with the Slovak Army. In German service, the LT vz.35s designated as Panzerkampfwagen 35(t) (t for Tschechisch-Czech). The LT-35 was comparable to German PzKpfw III and in 1939 was a vital addition to the Panzerwaffe. Despite a Czech decision to phase the LT-35 out of production after 1938, it was extended until 1939, under German supervision at the CKD (Ceskomoravska Kolben Danek) Works in Prague and the Skoda Works in Pilsen (after 1938 both became part of Reichswerke Hermann Goring).

Overall 424 were produced between 1935 and 1939 by Skoda (approx. 340) and CKD (approx. 84). PzKpfw 35(t) formed the bulk of the 1st Leichte (Light) Division during the Polish Campaign and then the 6th Panzer Division (formerly the 1st Leichte Division) during the French Campaign and the Invasion of Russia.

Panzer 35(t) in France, 1940

PzKpfw 35(t)s took part in the Polish (1939) and French campaign (1940) and in the early stages of the invasion of Russia (1941). During Operation Barbarossa the PzKpfw 35(t) was seen to he badly outclassed and of little value under combat conditions. Under winter conditions, the PzKpfw 35(t)'s mechanical components proved to be once again unreliable particularly as the clutch, brake and steering were all operated by compressed air. The LT-35(t)'s construction was riveted and a direct hit on its armour plate could sheer rivet heads off which would fly around inside the vehicle and kill or wound the crew. In late 1941, Germans had better tanks in production and the PzKptfw 35(t) was relocated to second line duties such as policing and anti partisan units. Some PzKpfw 35(t) were handed over to the Slovak, Bulgarian (where they served until 1950s), Romanian. Hungarian and Italian armies or were used by the German Police and the anti-partisan units.

Following the introduction of PzKpfw 35(t) into German service, it became a base for a few conversions. In September of 1940, Skoda produced the design for T-13 tank based on LT-35 but it never entered production. In 1941, tests were carried out to convert PzKpfw 35(t) into a tropical version but were never concluded. Also from March of 1942 to 1943, 49 PzKpfw 35(t)s were converted into Morser Zugmittel 1 Artillerie Schlepper 35(t) - artillery tractors by removing the turret and upper part of the hull and fitting a canvas cover in their place. Some were also mounted with 12,000kg towing hook in the rear. Others were cannibalised and saw service with coastal batteries. In 1939/40, designers tried to utilize the LT-35 chassis as the basis for a Panzerjäger 35(t), armed with the Skoda 47mm Pak 36(t) U43 (Skoda 47mm A5 gun) gun. This design never entered production and only two prototypes based on Morser Zugmittel 35(t) were produced and were in service until late 1943. Some 20 were converted to Befehlswagen 35(t) - command tanks fitted with additional radio equipment. A few other support or auxiliary vehicles were based on the LT-35 chassis and were produced in limited numbers. Most of the PzKpfw 35(t)'s turrets were used for fixed fortifications on the Danish coast and in Corsica.

In mid 1943, a team directed by Lt. Col. Constantin Ghiulai designed a self-propelled anti-tank gun designated T. A. C. A. M. Skoda R-2 for the Romanian army. A small series was produced at Leonida factory. Some sources state that as many as 40 were made. It was armed with captured Soviet ZIS-3 and F-22 UWS 76.2mm L/42 gun based on the modified PzKpfw 35 design. The gun was mounted in an open at the top and rear lightly armoured superstructure (made using armour plates from captured vehicles). The superstructure was mounted in the frontal part of the hull (in the place of the turret), while other components and characteristics remained unchanged. Overall the design of T. A. C. A. M. was similar to that of the German Marder series mirroring its high profile and light protection. Only 30 rounds were carried along with two machine guns for local defence for the crew of three men. The vehicle weighted 11500kg, had a range of 190km on the road and maximum speed of 34km/h. Due to the difficulties with 76.2mm ammunition, plans were made to utilize the German 88mm Pak 43 L/70 or Romanian 75mm Resita model 1943 gun but were never realized. T. A. C. A. M.s never saw service when Romania was Germany's ally and were only used against the Germans. Today, one T. A. C. A. M. Skoda R-2 can be seen in the museum in Bucharest. Romania. In addition, to T. A. C. A. M. Skoiti R-2, there was also variant based on captured Soviet T-60 light tank, designated T. A. C. A. M. T-60, of which some 35 were produced.

In 1940, Hungary purchased two examples and the licence from Skoda to produce S-IIc: (T-22) medium tank - an improved model of the LT-35 light tank. From 1942 to 1944, Hungarians produced Turan I (40M) medium tank, which was a modified version of T-22. It was then followed by Turan II (41 M) produced from 1943 to 1944 and prototype of Turan III in 1944. In addition, Zrinyi (40/43M) assault guns based on the Turan were produced in 1943. The Turan I was armed with a 40mm L/51 gun. The Turan II with a 75mm U25 gun and the Zrinyi with a 105mm L/20.5 howitzer. The prototype of Turan III was armed with a 75mm U43 gun, while there were also plans to arm the Zrinyi with the same gun. All designs were used by the Hungarian Army.

Overall, Panzerkampfwagen 35(t)s were reliable vehicles and served Panzertruppe very well in the time of need. Today, PzKpfw 35(t)s can be seen in the museums in Belgrade (Serbia), Bucharest (Romania.), Sofia (Bulgaria). Aberdeen (USA), while the LT vz.35 can be seen in Slovakia.

Armour (mm/angle) 35(t)
Front Turret: 25/10
Front Upper Hull: 25/17
Front Lower Hull: 25/30
Side Turret: 15/14
Side Upper Hull: 16/0
Side Lower Hull: 16/0
Rear Turret: 15/15
Rear Upper Hull: 15/60
Rear Lower Hull: 16/0
Turret Top/ Bottom: 8/81
Upper Hull Top / Bottom: 8/85
Lower Hull Top / Bottom: 8/90
Gun Mantlet: 25/round

Model	35(t)
Weight	10,500 kg
Crew	4
Engine	Skoda T 11 / 6-cylinder 120 bhp
Speed	35 km/h
Range	Road: 190 km Crosscountry: 120 km
Length	4.90 m
Width	2.10 m
Height	2.35 m
Armament	37 mm KwK 34(t) L/40 (Skoda 37 mm A3 vz. 34) 2 x 7.92 mm MG34 or MG35/37(t)
Ammunition Supply	37 mm - 72 to 90 rounds 7.92 mm - 1800 to 2550 rounds

The (35)t provided a valuable influx of strength at a time when the German Panzer forces desperately needed extra machines to match the ambitious expansion programme.

37 mm Kwk 34(t) L/40 Penetration of armour plate at 30 degrees from vertical					
Ammunition	100 m	500 m	1000 m	1500 m	2000 m
Panzergranate 39	37 mm	31 mm	26 mm	22 mm	0 mm
Pzgr. 39 (APCBC) - Armour Piercing Composite Ballistic Cap					
Pzgr. 40 (APCR) - Armour Piercing Composite Rigid (Tungsten Core)					

CONVERSIONS

- **Zugkraftwagen 35(t)** - light artillery tractor
- **Munitionsschlepper 35(t)** - ammunition carrier
- **Morser Zugmittel / Artillerie Schlepper 35(t)** - artillery tractor
- **Panzerjäger 35(t)** - 47mm Pak 36(t) L/43 carrier
- **Befehlswagen 35(t)** - command tank

The strategy that had eventually been settled upon for the attack was of breath taking audacity.

A surprise offensive was launched through Holland and Belgium which it was hoped would draw the allied forces northwards away from their entrenched defensive positions in France. Then a powerful concentration of German armour would crash through the weakly defended Ardennes region. Without real opposition, this arm of the attack would thrust into France to tear the allied armies in half.

FALL GELB ACTIVATED

Soon after the attack was launched it was obvious that the great stratagem was working immaculately and it was reported that when Hitler was told, he almost wept for joy.

To the south, the seven armoured German divisions leading the principal offensive were feeling their way through the Ardennes.

Believing a passage to be impossible here, and, relying on the massive fortifications of the Maginot Line, the French had largely neglected this region, and the Germans had to contend with little more than a bemused Belgian horse soldier, peering incomprehensibly through the trees.

Although the French airmen observed the German movement, their reports were ignored, so the vast assemblage edged on unhampered towards the river Meuse and France.

The river Meuse was the one great obstacle confronting the invaders. It was reached on the morning of 13th May. Despite skirmishes, the defenders still remained in ignorance of the scale of the impending onslaught. Away to the north a large clash of French and German armour confirmed the allied command in their mistaken analysis of German intentions.

The Meuse was to be crossed at three points. Exploiting German air superiority, the defenders at Sedan were subjected to an intensive bombardment lasting six hours. It was a murderous onslaught, and Guderian's engineers crossed the river swiftly afterwards, followed by the first infantry.

By evening, the Germans had smashed their way across and were on the other side in strength, having at last broken the shattered French forces. The two other crossings had also been successfully forced, a crippling blow to the whole allied defence.

In front of the Germans lay long stretches of ideal tank country held mainly by poorly trained, ill-equipped and elderly reservists. The flying artillery of the dive bombers was already at work

A German tank crew perch on the hulk of a knocked out French tank during the early phases of the French campaign.

wreaking wholesale destruction and inspiring widespread terror. Behind the spearheads extending back from the Meuse nearly to the Rhine itself, crowded the 25 divisions of the supporting infantry.

That same day, 15th May 1940, Holland surrendered.

On the following day, as the breach ripped in the southern French defences widened dramatically, it was belatedly apparent to the allied command that a potential catastrophe was in the making. The slow, clumsy bombers sent against German targets were sharply repulsed. The armies, attempting to make a hasty retreat from the Lowlands, found the roads choked with panic-stricken refugees.

For transmission of orders and reports, the allied command relied heavily on despatch riders and on the telephone network. Except that now, neither could be relied upon. In the aftermath of invasion, hundreds of French aircraft had been hurriedly removed to safe locations, and no one could find them. The skies were becoming the unchallenged domain of the Luftwaffe.

In many allied units morale and discipline were evaporating. The twin German spearheads thrust on, piercing deeper into France.

The most significant advance was made by the 7th Panzer Division commanded by General Erwin Rommel. His tank force advanced quickly through the lightly defended areas in Belgium. When they ran into heavier defended areas in France, they used their speed, surprise and weight of fire to overwhelm the enemy. This unit became the first to cross the river Mouse. Once across, they continued their advance towards Arras. The 7th Panzer Division was advancing so fast that they were given the unofficial nickname of the 'Ghost Division'. The 'Ghost Division' had good reason to celebrate Hitler's Czechoslovakian adventure. They were mostly equipped with 38(t) tanks.

THE COUNTER ATTACK AT ARRAS

When the 7th Panzer Division advanced further they came into the area held by a mixed British and French force. The British, who were to the north of the German advance, decided to mount a counter-attack from the direction of Arras. They were under the impression that the French, who were south of the German advance, would also attack. On 21 May the British launched their attack into the flank of the Germans.

The allied force was small in comparison to the German forces, but they put up a good fight and actually caused a panic in the German High Command. Elements of the 7th Panzer Division were redirected back towards Arras to meet the threat. The Germans had estimated the attacking allied force to number hundreds of tanks when, in fact, it was considerably less than this. Although the British attack was determined, a French thrust from the south failed to materialise and the battle could not halt the advance of the enemy. It did, however, give the Germans a bloody nose and cause them considerable concern. This attack had showed what could be achieved if the allies had been better coordinated.

Guderian's amazing sweep from the Meuse to the sea exemplified Blitzkrieg in its purest and most lethally efficient form. Urged on by their impetuous commander and to the increasing alarm of some his superiors, his tanks drove onward to the coast, frequently covering 50 miles a day and far outstripping the supporting infantry. Often the mere sight and sound of the thundering tanks was sufficient to disperse any opposition.

The disaster at Sedan caused consternation among the French High Command. Astute French officers had read correctly the lessons of Poland. Tragically, their Generals suffered from the military equivalent of myopia and blithely ignored them. New technology had been accepted only grudgingly, new ideas, never. In the long, cumbrous chains of command, it could easily take two days for an order to reach the front, by which time the battle situation was usually completely transformed.

Guderian's tanks drove relentlessly on. All over France wild rumours abounded: of fifth-columnists and saboteurs, of bizarrely-disguised German paratroopers, of imminent new disasters. The already prevalent mood of defeatism deepened further.

A Panzer III rumbles by a dispirited British soldier in the wake of the allied collapse in Greece.

Yet the French had more troops than the Germans and a superiority in nearly all types of armaments. They even had more tanks than the Germans, and the best of them, such as the heavily armed Chars and Somuas, were formidable vehicles of war.

What were missing were the will and the perception to use all of these advantages in a concentrated approach to modern warfare. It would have required an impossibly drastic shift in the thinking of the past 50 years. Quarrels between French and British, inter-service rivalries and other dangerous pettiness combined further to make an effective military response impossible.

On 20th May Guderian reached Amiens. The last link between the allied forces to the north and south was severed, adding still further to the already dire confusion in the chain of command.

On the 24th Hitler issued one of the most controversial orders of the war. For two days the tanks were halted. This respite prevented a massacre taking place during the subsequent evacuation of BEF from Dunkirk. This has been one of the most hotly debated actions of the war and numerous possible reasons have been ascribed to Hitler's curious order. One very plausible explanation is that Hitler, from his studies of the rates of attrition of the tank forces, had become concerned that his armoured forces would be too worn down to continue the battle against France.

Throughout his military career Hitler was inclined to dabble in every aspect of detail, even to the point of inspecting the daily strength returns for the Panzer Divisions. There is a strong possibility that he may have confused the numbers of unserviceable machines, which could be repaired in the very short term, with those that were complete write-offs. The lessons from the street fighting in Warsaw may also have had an impact. With the withdrawal of the BEF, France now faced the mighty German forces alone. They were unable to hold back the tide of men and weapons.

Once Dunkirk was secured the Germans surveyed the mayhem that had been left behind by the retreating BEF. The British had been forced to abandon all of their equipment and the majority of this lay in ruin around the port. The German victory was not yet complete and the next phase required them to turn south and concentrate on the remaining French and British forces that still numbered some 66 Divisions. This part of the advance began on 5th June 1940. Less than 3 weeks later the enemy was completely defeated.

By 10th June, with the Germans outside the French capital, the government abandoned Paris. Widespread fighting continued but there was no place for illusions. A full-scale rout was taking place.

On 20th June, after just six weeks of war, France agreed to sign a demeaning armistice.

Hitler was overjoyed at this astounding vindication of the methods of Blitzkrieg. Germany rejoiced with him and with the glorious euphoria of victory mingled a deeper, more human desire. For the German population the war was surely over. The nation's honour had been restored, German prosperity assured by the new order in Europe. The ignominy of Versailles was lost in the past. Under their revered leader this transformation had been achieved at a cost far below all expectation.

The Armistice was signed by the leaders of the destroyed French forces in the same railway carriage that they themselves had used at the end of the First World War. This was the perfect end to what was almost a perfect victory for Hitler and his new Panzer army.

The part played by the German tanks in the victory had been crucial. In a few weeks they had destroyed the armies of Holland, Belgium, France and Britain. The confidence of the Germans was at an all time high. They had complete faith in their men and machines. The close support of the Luftwaffe had also been a deciding factor and helped to instil terror upon the fleeing enemy soldiers. Hitler now regarded the war as almost won. New weapons development was restricted after this time due to the strains on the economy and resources were routed to anti-tank weapons and the more economical assault guns. The deficiencies that were apparent with regard to armour protection and main armament in these early campaigns were to resurface in later campaigns, but with greater consequences. The best that Germany could offer in 1941 would be severely outclassed by the Russian tanks.

With a sense of invincibility in everyone's mind, a complacency and lack of urgency set in. Although Hitler was already looking to undertake the biggest gamble yet, the equipment of the tank forces did not undergo any serious redesign. It is true to say that an expansion programme was undertaken that was to add many new units to Germany's armed forces, but there was no real thought given to imputing the existing tools of destruction. Minor modifications were made to the Panzer III which had the main gun upgraded to a 50mm weapon and a slight increase in armour thickness. The Panzer IV also had the armour increased slightly, to 50mm. The expansion programme also had to cater for the units that needed their battle losses replaced. German tanks required hundreds of man-hours to complete; this meant they were comparatively slow to come off the production line compared to the Russian T-34s that were simple and cheap to produce.

Other experiments were conducted in preparation for the proposed invasion of England, code named Operation Sea Lion. One of the most interesting was the development of a submersible Panzer III. Although the planned invasion did not materialise, this development would be used in the early stages of Operation Barbarossa. Hitler, although annoyed at the failure of the Luftwaffe to deliver victory against England, plunged ahead with the planning for the mighty invasion of the Soviet Union. He was confident that his army would deliver victory once more. The men on the front line would quickly discover just how inadequate their tanks would be against the enemy. The puny 37mm gun was still used to equip many of the Panzer Ills, which were then Germany's main battle tanks. The same 37mm gun was also carried by all of the Czech made 38(t) tanks which, in 1940, were Germany's most numerous battle tanks. These guns were insufficient to penetrate at all but the shortest range, and even the upgrade to a 50mm gun carried by some Panzer III by 1941 was still not really sufficient.

Only the 75mm gun of the Panzer IV and Sturmgeschütze battalions were really suited to the demands of the modern battlefield, even then it had its limitations. The short barrel of the 75mm gave the shells only a limited velocity, which was effective against the thinly armoured tanks of the early war years but proved to be totally inadequate when the Germans met the superior Russian tanks during 1941.

CAPTURED TANKS

As we have seen, during the Second World War the German Army utilised large numbers of captured tanks; the trend had already been established after the Polish campaign. The German Armed Forces now captured and confiscated a far more significant haul of armoured fighting vehicles, many of which were pressed into service by the Wehrmacht, Waffen-SS, Luftwaffe and Police units. These Beute Panzerkampfwagen (captured Panzers) were gathered at special collection points, where they were examined for any potential benefits to the new owners. If possible, useful tanks were returned to the factories where they had been built and repaired, modified and painted in German colours and markings.

As of October 1940 the German Army Office requested that, if possible, two examples of every captured vehicle were to be provided for evaluation at the Kummersdorf (Motor Vehicle Test Centre of the Army Weapons Office's Test Section) and Berka (tank school) facilities. Eventually, after all tests had been concluded, they were moved to the Tank Museum of the Army Vehicle Office in Stettin-Altdamm (now Szczecin). These tests determined the combat value of various tanks and provided information on their general characteristics, along with shooting tests that were summarised in firing tables. In the desperate days of March 1945, the High Command of the Army Group Vistula authorised the captured tanks from the museum to be used in

PANZERKAMPFWAGEN 38(T) SD.KFZ.140

The LT (Light Tank) vz. (model) 38 was destined to become one of the most widely used Czechoslovak tanks, although not in Czechoslovak hands. Ordered into production in 1938, the LT-3S drew on the experience of many countries and gained an excellent reputation among its foreign users such as Sweden (THN Sv), Iran / Persia (TNH), Peru (LTP), Switzerland (LTH - Pz39) and Lithuania (LTL).

The 1938/39 German take-over of the Czechoslovak state meant that in March 1939. 150 LT-38s in production were confiscated and CKD/Praga was ordered to complete them. All of these machines were incorporated into the German Army as PzKpfw 38(t) Ausf A - Sd.Kfz. 140. After the German take-over of the Czechoslovakia, the LT-38 became one of the most important tanks used by the Panzertruppe and was retained in production as a battle tank until June of 1942. During the war, PzKpfw 38(t) were exported and saw service with German allies including: Romania (50). Slovakia (90), Bulgaria (10) and Hungary (102). The PzKpfw 38(t) also saw service with the allies. A single tank was captured by British and French troops in May / June 1940, another example (turret number - 543) was captured either during the Italian Campaign in 1943 or Normandy in 1944 and was tested in England. Numbers of PzKpfw 38(t)s were captured and pressed into service by the Red Army. Finally, in May of 1945, PzKpfw 38(t) now known as LT-38137 (37 standing for 37mm gun) was back in service with the Czechoslovak Army as a training tank until the early 1950s.

Approximately 1,400 PzKpfw 38(t)s were produced in 8 different variants (Ausf A/B/C/D/E/F/S/G) with various modifications and improved armour protection. All were armed with Czech made 37mm Skoda A7 vz.38 guns designated by the Germans as 37mm

Panzer 38(t), Soviet Union, June 1941

KwK 38(t) U48 (L/47.8). In early models construction was riveted, and a direct hit on its armour plate could sheer off rivet heads which would kill or wound the crew. Later model construction was largely welded. Late models were further up-armoured and a few were possibly rearmed with German made 37mm KwK 35/36 L/46.5 gun. A number were also converted to flamethrower tanks by replacing the hull machine gun with a flamethrower, with fuel supplied from a towed single-axle trailer carrying 200 litres of fuel linked by a flexible hose. There was also a PzKpfW 38(t) swimming tank with a prototype AP-1 float but it never entered production. Further production of the PzKpfw 38(t) chassis continued with improved models of Ausf H/K/L/M, which were used as a base for various vehicles (such as the Marder III Ausf H/M, Bison/Grille Ausf H/K/M and Hetzer). In addition, older models returned for repairs were often also used as a base for a conversion.

PzKpfw 38(t)s were built under German supervision and they saw extensive service in Poland (3rd Leichte Division), Norway (XXXI Armee Korps), France (6th, 7th and 8th Panzer Divisions), Balkans (8th Panzer Division) and Russia (6th, 7th, 8th, 12th, 19th and 20th Panzer Divisions). During the fighting in Russia, the need for heavier armour and armament rendered the PzKpfw 38(t) inadequate and in 1942 it was relegated to second line duties (e.g. reconnaissance and service in armoured trains).

In September of 1939 plans were laid for the development of a fast/light reconnaissance tank. 15 PzKpfw 38(t) nA (neuer Art) were produced by BMM (Praga/CKD) in early 1942, but its design was not accepted for production. In 1942, the usual German process of adapting the chassis for other purposes commenced with the Marder III and Flakpanzer 38(t). In 1942 and 1943 a number of PzKpfw 38(t) had their turrets removed and were converted to driver training vehicles; late in the war they were mounted with wood burning generators. Training vehicles based on turretless tanks were designated as PzKpfw 38(t) Schulfahrwanne and were used by school units of the Wehrmacht and NSKK. Some 351 PzKpfw 38(t) turrets were used for German fortifications in Norway (75), Denmark (20), the Western Atlantic shore (9). Italy (25). Southwest Europe (150) and Eastern Europe (78).

Armour (mm/angle) Ausfuhrung A	Armour (mm/angle) Ausfuhrung G
Front Turret: 25/10	Front Turret: 50/10
Front Upper Hull: 25/17	Front Upper Hull: 50/17
Front Lower Hull: 25/16	Front Lower Hull: 50/16
Side Turret: 15/10	Side Turret: 30/10
Side Upper Hull: 15/0	Side Upper Hull: 15+15/0
Side Lower Hull: 15/0	Side Lower Hull: 15/0
Rear Turret: 15/10	Rear Turret: 22/10
Rear Upper Hull: 10/60	Rear Upper Hull: 10/60
Rear Lower Hull: 15/12	Rear Lower Hull: 15/12
Turret Top/ Bottom: 10/90	Turret Top/ Bottom: 15/90
Upper Hull Top / Bottom: 8/90	Upper Hull Top / Bottom: 8/90
Lower Hull Top / Bottom: 8/90	Lower Hull Top / Bottom: 8/90
Gun Mantlet: 25/round	Gun Mantlet: 25/round

The 38(t) was to prove an acceptable stop-gap which gave the Panzerwaffe an alternative to the Panzer III which was slow to arrive in large numbers.

Model	Ausfuhrung A	Ausfuhrung G
Weight	9400 kg	9850 kg
Crew	4	4
Engine	Praga EPA / 6-cylinder 125 bhp	Praga EPA / 6-cylinder 125 bhp
Speed	Road: 42 km/h Crosscountry: 15 km/h	Road: 42 km/h Crosscountry: 15 km/h
Range	Road: 250 km Crosscountry: 160 km	Road: 250 km Crosscountry: 160 km
Length	4.60 m	4.61 m
Width	2.12 m	2.14 m
Height	2.40 m	2.40 m
Armament	37 mm KwK 38(t) L/47.8 2 x 7.92 mm MG37(t)	37 mm KwK 38(t) L/47.8 2 x 7.92 mm MG37(t)
Ammunition Supply	37 mm - 72 rounds 7.92 mm - 2400 rounds	37 mm - 42 rounds 7.92 mm - 2400 rounds

37 mm Kwk 38(t) L/47.8 Penetration of armour plate at 30 degrees from vertical					
Ammunition	100 m	500 m	1000 m	1500 m	2000 m
Panzergranate 39	41 mm	35 mm	29 mm	24 mm	0 mm
Panzergranate 40	64 mm	34 mm	0 mm	0 mm	0 mm
Pzgr. 39 (APCBC) - Armour Piercing Composite Ballistic Cap					
Pzgr. 40 (APCR) - Armour Piercing Composite Rigid (Tungsten Core)					

CONVERSIONS

- **Bison (Grille) Ausf. H/M** - 15cm s.IG. (Sd. Kfz. 138/1) - howitzer carrier
- **Munitionspanzer 38(t) Ausf M** - ammunition carrier
- **Schutzenpanzerwagen 38(t) Ausf M** - armoured personal carrier (planned)
- **Marder III (Sd. Kfz. 139)** - 76.2 mm Pak 36 (Russian) gun
- **Marder III Ausf. H/K/M (Sd. Kfz. 138)** - 75 mm Pak 40 gun
- **Befehlswagen 38(t)** - command tank
- **Munitionsschlepper 38(t)** - ammuntion carrier
- **Panzerjäger 38(t) / Jagedpanzer 38(t) Hetzer**
- **Pz.Kpfw. 38(t) nA** - fast/light reconnaissance tank

The lightning invasions of Poland, France, Holland and Belgium were made possible by the unexpected addition to the Panzerwaffe of the 38(t).

On campaign with the "flying ghost" Division. This shot from Signal magazine displays the daily life of the 11th Panzer Division on campaign in France and the Balkans.

the defence of Stettin. Some of the foreign captured tanks were put in the active service with special captured tank units (formed from May 1940), others were allocated to Panzer or Infantry Divisions in various roles, such as reconnaissance. Some units, for example Panzer Abteilung 216 in the Channel Islands and the 7th SS-Freiwilligen-Gebirgs-Division 'Prinz Eugen' in the Balkans were totally equipped with captured equipment.

According to original German captured tank inventories as of 10th April 1945, there were still 424 captured tanks in German service, 71 on the Eastern Front, 172 in Italy, 74 in the Balkans and 107 in Norway and Denmark: of these 310 were Operational. In general, the most common practice was the conversion of foreign tanks into various weapon carriers. Some tanks were also converted into other supplementary vehicles, such as artillery tractors. Foreign tanks were mainly used for training purposes, while some were used for internal policing duties in occupied territories (Polizei-Panzerkampfwagen). Field modifications were very common and totally non-standard. The most common modification to tanks was the replacement of the original cupola top with split hatch covers and the installation of radio equipment.

In order to identify and classify captured and foreign equipment. Foreign Equipment Listing (D.50) series - Kennblaetter Fremdengerat - was published. It consisted of 14 volumes (updated during the course of war) and captured motor vehicles were listed in the twelfth volume (D.50/12). All vehicles were divided into seven numerical block categories:

200 for armoured cars
300 for half-tracked (semi-tracked) vehicles
400 for armoured half-tracked (semi-tracked) vehicles
600 for fully-tracked artillery tractors
630 for armoured artillery tractors
700 for tanks (including British armoured carriers)
800 for gun carriers and self-propelled guns

In addition, letters followed numbers. Letters were used to recognise the previous user (not producer) of a certain piece of the equipment. For example Soviet T-34 was designated as Panzerkampfwagen T-34 747(r).

(a) amerikanisch - American
(b) belgisch - Belgium
(c) englisch - English and Canadian
(d) französisch - French
(h) hollandisch - Dutch
(i) italienisch - Italian
(j) jugoslawisch - Yugoslavian
(o) osterreichisch - Austrian
(p) polnisch - Polish
(r) russisch - Russian
(t) tschechisch - Czechoslovakian

CAPTURED TANKS IN GERMAN HANDS

After their victory in Western Europe, Germans pressed captured British equipment into service, and some examples remained as late as 1945.

The Belgian Army had some one hundred and fifty Vickers Carden-Loyd Mark I 'Dragon' (export version) light tanks designated as Char Leger Modele T.

In addition, there were some seventy-five Renault FT-17/18 two-man light tanks, but there is no evidence of them being used by the Germans, although it is possible that they were classified as Dutch or French FT series tanks.

The main haul of captured enemy tanks to fall into German hands came after the fall of France. During the course of the French Campaign the Germans captured approximately 2.400 out of the 3,500 French tanks in service as of 10th May 1940. On 30th August 1941 Hitler issued an order that all captured equipment was to be used to equip Panzer Divisions newly formed in France. Captured tanks were issued to the four Panzer Regiments numbered from 201 to 204; these regiments were equipped entirely with captured tanks, additional machines were transferred to Panzer Abteilung z.b.V (special employment units), which included Panzer Regiments 100, 202 to 205, 211 to 214 and 223 Panzer Abteilung. In addition there were numerous captured tank platoons. The majority of those units operated in occupied territories, especially the Balkans, where they performed internal policing and security duties.

CAPTURED FRENCH TANKS

The oldest captured tank in German service was the Renault FT-17/18 (FT - Faible Tonnage - Light Weight) two-man light tank, designated by the victorious Germans as Panzerkampfwagen 17R/18R 730(f). The French Army still had some eight hundred examples of this antiquated machine which dated in its design back to early 1917. It was produced in numerous versions and widely exported to Belgium, Czechoslovakia, Finland, Holland, Yugoslavia and Poland. It was recognised as having no front line combat value upon its capture by the Germans and many of the captured tanks badly needed repairs. Nonetheless, some were still used for training, policing and security duties in the Channel Islands. Germany. Norway and Serbia. Others were used as command and artillery posts. Some were converted to artillery tractors by having the upper part of the hull, along with the turret removed.

The remaining FT-17/18s were used in armoured trains or were handed over to the Luftwaffe to be used for security duties and as snow ploughs for their airfields. Some were still in use as late as 1945. According to original German captured tank inventories as of July 1943, there were still 12FT-17/18 tanks in active service in the West, mainly France. Some tanks took part in the Paris rising of August 1944, being used both by the Germans and the uprisers.

The Renault VM/AMR 33 (1933) and Renault ZT/AMR 35 (1935) were two-man light cavalry tanks. Again, they had little

A column of Panzer II tanks halts for a well-earned rest during the Balkan campaign. The movement of armoured formations by road was an extremely complex logistical undertaking.

combat value and were mainly used for police duties in occupied territories. In German service, AMR 33 was designated as Panzerspahwagen VM 70l(f).

The Renault Char Leger R-35 two-man light tanks were the most numerous French tanks as of May 1940 and approximately eight hundred and forty (out of 1,035 in service) were captured by the Germans. The Renault R-35 was designated as Panzerkampfwagen 35R 731(f).

The R-35 was a reasonable design. Some R-35s in France were even pressed into German service during the course of the campaign in France. After the campaign, repaired vehicles were modified to German standards by replacing the original cupola top with split hatch covers and the addition or replacement of radio equipment.

Although R-35s and R-40s were not obsolete vehicles, their characteristics made them unsuitable for front line service and only a small number were used as infantry support tanks. The majority were relegated to second line duties in Western Europe. Some twenty-five Renault R-35s served with the Panzer Abteilung z.b.V 12 (special employment unit) and were used in an anti-partisan role in the Balkans: another 30 were handed over to the SS and were used for policing duties in occupied territories.

In late 1941 46 R-35s were also used to equip the 100th Panzerbrigade, which was the basis of the newly formed 21st Panzer Division of North Africa fame. The R-35s were not taken to Africa and after the debacle in Tunisia the same machines were used for training the nucleus of the new division again in late 1943. Panzer Abteilung 206, which operated in the Cherbourg peninsula in June 1944, is known to have used two R-35s in action. A Number of R-35s also saw service with 100th Panzer Ersatz und Ausbildung Abteilung (reserve Tank Battalion), which was supporting the 96th Infantry Division in St. Lo - Caretan area in June 1944. In addition, some were also used by units stationed in the Channel Islands along with the garrison in Paris. Some unmodified tanks were also used in armoured trains.

In 1940 Germans handed over 109 R-35s to Italy, where they equipped two reserve tank battalions but proved to be useless due to the lack of spare parts. Undeterred, in 1941 the Germans sold some forty R-35s to their Bulgarian allies, where they equipped the 1st Armoured Brigade that performed security duties in Serbia until September 1944, although the Bulgarians must surely have encountered similar difficulties to the Italians.

From May to October 1941, Alkett in Berlin converted 174 R-35s to anti-tank hunters. Designated as '4.7cm Pak(t) auf Panzerkampfwagen 35R(t') ohne Turm' or Panzerjäger 35R 731(f), it was intended to replace the inefficient Panzerjäger I. These machines equipped the second-string tank destroyer units of Infantry Divisions. Interestingly, there were still some one

The Germans felt they had little to gain from the employment of many of the French tanks captured in the wake of the fall of France. These light tanks are being employed for ploughing duties, a purpose to which many were better suited than combat.

hundred and ten in service in France as of early 1944, and 20 remained in service as late as May 1945 in the Channel Islands.

A number of R-35s escaped the conversion process and remained in service with garrison infantry units and in 1945 there were still a few Panzerkampfwagen 35R 73 1 (f) in German service. According to original German captured tank inventories, as of July 1943 there were 58 R-35s in service in the West.

The Renault Char D-1 infantry (medium) tanks were designated by the Germans as Panzerkampfwagen D-1 732(f). Although the Germans captured a number there is no evidence of them being pressed into service. As of 10 May 1940 the French Army had some seventy-five D-2s in service, although it can be assumed that few were used for security duties or as mobile fortifications. It is most likely the majority were scrapped and their turrets were handed over to Croatia, where they were mounted on armoured trains.

A total of 1,188 Hotchkiss tanks were in service with the French Army as of 10th May 1940: of these, the Germans captured approximately six hundred. Generally, all Hotchkiss tanks were referred to as Panzerkampfwagen 38H 735(f).

The Germans modified Hotchkiss tanks to their standards by replacing the original cupola top with split hatch covers and by the addition or replacement of radio equipment. Hotchkiss tanks were issued to captured tank Panzer Regiments of various Panzer Divisions (including the 7th and 8th in late 1940) as battle tanks, and saw service in France, Norway, Crete, the Balkans, Finland and

Russia. The first unit to be equipped with Hotchkiss tanks and which saw combat in Finland in the summer of 1941 was Panzer Abteilung 211. Some Hotchkiss tanks also equipped the 100th and 101st Beute-Panzer-Brigades. Hotchkiss tanks were also used in a reconnaissance role, as command tanks. Some tanks, including some sixty in service with the SS, were used for internal policing and security duties. The Germans also handed over 15 Hotchkiss tanks to Hungary in 1943 and sold 19 to Bulgaria in 1944. Two H-39s were handed over to Croatia. As of 20th May 1942 there were 15 Hotchkiss tanks with Panzer Abteilung 212 stationed on Crete.

Twenty-four Hotchkiss tanks were converted to communication and command tanks designated as Ein Grosser Funk und Befehlswagen 38H 735(f), also known as Artillerie-Panzer-Beobaehtung 38H 735(f), artillery observation vehicles. All 24 were issued to 21st Panzer Division's 155th Panzerartillerie Abteilung stationed in France in 1944.

In 1942, some twenty-four (some sources state sixty) H-39s (including at least one H-JJ) were converted to 75mm PaK 40 L/46 anti-tank gun carriers (Panzerjäger), designated as '7.5cm PaK40 (Sf) auf Geschutzwagen 39H(f)' but more commonly referred to as Marder I. A similar conversion was also completed in 1942 by converting 48 H-39s to 105mm leFH 16 L/22 and leFH 18 (18/40) L/28 (leichte Feldhaubitze - light field howitzer) carriers, designated as '10.5cm leFH18(Sf) auf Geschutzwagen 39H(f)'. In both conversions armament was mounted in an open-topped superstructure. Both conversions were completed by Captain Alfred Becker's Baukommando in Paris and at Krefeld (in co-operation with Alkett in Berlin) and served with units stationed in France, including 8th Panzerartillerie Abteilung and Sturmgeschütz Abteilung 200, commanded by Major Alfred Becker. The turrets of vehicles converted to weapon carriers were used in fortifications; some tanks were even dug in as fixed bunkers.

Another interesting conversion were 11 H-35s and H-38s mounted with '428 32cm schwere Wuhrframen 40' (28O/320mm rocket projector) by Panzer Abteilung 205.

Some Hotchkiss tanks were also used in armoured trains operating in the Balkans. As late as 1944 some were also used as training vehicles with their turrets and hatches removed. It was also a common practice to equip units refitting and resting in France with captured tanks for the duration of their time in the field. (The 6th Panzer Division's Panzer Regiment II was equipped in this way). As of 31 May 1943 there were 355 captured tanks in German service. According to original German captured tank inventories, as of July 1943, they were distributed as follows: 15 as part of Army Group Centre, 96 in the Balkans, 149 in the West, 68 in Norway and 33 in Lapland. Panzer Abteilung 206, which operated in the Cherbourg peninsula in June of 1944, used sixteen H-38s. A number of H-38s also saw service with the 100th Panzer Ersatz und Ausbildung

This unusual photograph demonstrates the lengths to which the German propaganda service were prepared to go to achieve results. The lens of a camera has replaced the machine-gun of this Panzer III.

Abteilung (Reserve Tank Battalion), which was supporting the 96th Infantry Division in the St. Lo-Caretan area in June 1944. As of 30th December 1944, there were still 29 (H-38s) Hotchkiss tanks in German service and even a few in 1945. At least one unarmed H-39 tank was captured and pressed into service by the insurgents during the Prague uprising in May 1945.

The Char de Cavalerie Somua S/35Char 1935 S three man medium tank armed with 47mm SA 35 L/34 gun and 7.5mm Reibel machine gun was the best French tank as of May of 1940 and around five hundred were in service with the French Army. It was the first vehicle in the world with all-cast hull and turret. This feature, however, made it unsuitable for conversion. Some Somuas were pressed into service during the campaign by the by 3rd SS (Motorised) Division, 'Totenkopf'. Altogether, during the course of campaign, the Germans captured two hundred and ninety-seven Somua S-35s, designated as Panzerkampfwagen 35S 739(f), and employed them mainly as commander's tanks along with some machine-gun armed command tanks with rear mounted frame antennas and additional radio equipment. The Germans modified S-35s to their standards by replacing original cupola top with split hatch covers and the addition or replacement of radio equipment. The first unit to be equipped with Somua tanks, which saw combat in Finland in the summer of 1941, was Panzer Abteilung 211. In 1941 Germans handed over some thirty-two S-35s to Italy, two to Hungary in 1943 and six to Bulgaria in 1944.

As of 20th May 1942 there were five Somua S-35 tanks with Panzer Abteilung 212 stationed on Crete.

In November 1941 some sixty Somuas had their turrets removed and were used as artillery tractors, along with ammunition carriers, on the Eastern Front. The turrets were used in fortifications on the Atlantic Wall.

Panzerkampfwagen 35S 739(f) tanks were issued to captured tank Panzer Regiments of various Panzer Divisions and saw service in France, Norway, the Balkans, Finland and Russia. S-35s were also used in equipping the newly formed 23d Panzer Division (France 1941/42) and the 24th Panzer Division, East Prussia, in late 1941.

On the eve of D-Day, on 1st June 1944, the 21st Panzer Division stationed in Normandy had twenty-three Somua S-35s in service. A number of S-35s also saw service with the 100th Panzer Ersatz und Ausbildung Abteilung (Reserve Tank Battalion), which was supporting the 96th Infantry Division in the St. Lo-Caretan area in June of 1944. According to original German captured tank inventories, as of July 1943 there were two S-35s as part of Army Group Centre, 43 in the Balkans, 67 in the West, 17 in Norway and 16 in Lapland. There were still some thirty S-35s in German service as of 30th December 1944 and few in 1945. Some of the 'German' Somuas were captured and ended up with the French resistance.

THE SUMA FLAME-THROWERS

The Germans designated the Renault Char De Bataille B-l (Char B) four-man heavy tanks as Panzerkampfwagen B-2 740(f). As of 10th May 1941 the French Army had some three hundred and seventy Char Bs in service and the Germans captured around one hundred and sixty of them. The Chars were altered to the German standards, along with some other minor modifications, but were not issued to troops as quickly as other captured tanks.

Sometimes fear alone is enough to overcome an enemy. This was certainly the case with flame-throwing tanks. These gruesome weapons had their main tank guns replaced with a flame-thrower which could fire a jet of flame for up to fifty yards. This was not a particularly accurate, or even an effective, weapon but both sides used them in the Second World War. They were designed to be used to winkle infantry out of strong defences, pillboxes and bunkers, but their main effectiveness lay in the fear they generated.

The flame gun fired an inflammable mixture from a 100-litre tank, which was enough to fire 80 two-second bursts of flame.

In March 1941 it was decided to convert a number of Chars to flame-thrower tanks and weapon carriers. From November 1941 to June 1942 some sixty Panzerkampfwagen B-2 740(f) tanks were converted to flame-thrower tanks, designated as Flammwagen auf Panzerkampfwagen B-2(f)/Flammpanzer 132(f). Conversion consisted of removal of the hull-mounted 75mm KwK 35(f) L/17 gun and replacement with Koebe's Flammenwerfer (flame-thrower). The flame-thrower had limited traverse of its own and the tank had to be pivoted to face the target.

This installation of the first flame-thrower was inefficient and was followed by a second model. In place of the original armament platform space was made for a special Spitzkoepf (as used in the Flammpanzer II), which housed the flame-thrower spray head and allowed it to operate at 180° radius. Along with this installation an additional visor was mounted in the frontal plate. Approximately twenty-five Chars were converted by Wegmann & Company at Kassel and Daimler-Benz in Berlin. These, along with six unmodified Chars, were issued to Panzer Abteilung (F) 102, and on 23rd June 1941 arrived on the front. In Russia Panzer Abteilung (F) 102 supported the 24th and 296th Infantry Divisions. It was not a successful baptism. On 27th June 1941 Panzer Abteilung (F) 102 was disbanded and further development of flame-thrower mounts took place. A final version was now introduced, which consisted of installing a ball-mounted flame-thrower in the mantlet fixed in the location of the original armament, along with an extension of the fighting compartment. Thirty-six Chars were converted in this way, and previously converted Chars were also rebuilt to this standard.

As of 31st May 1943 the 223rd Panzer Company on the Eastern Front had four Chars and twelve flame-thrower Chars, while 7th SS-Freiwillingen-Gebirgs-Division 'Prinz Eugen' in Yugoslavia had 7 regular Chars and 10 flame-thrower Chars. In addition, the 101 Panzer Brigade in France had 10 regular Chars and 24 flame-thrower Chars, and Panzer Abteilung 213 in the Channel Islands had 10 flame-thrower Chars (5 on Jersey and 5 on Guernsey) and 26 Chars (12 on Jersey and 14, including 2 command tanks, on Guernsey). Panzer Abteilung 206, which operated in the Cherbourg peninsula in June 1944, used five Chars. A Number of Chars also saw service with 100th Panzer Ersatz und Ausbildung Abteilung (Reserve Tank Battalion), which was supporting the 96th Infantry Division in the St. Lo-Caretan area in June 1944.

Following the conversion of Chars to flame-thrower tanks in 1942, 16 were converted to 105mm leFH 18/39 L/28 (leichte Feldhaubitze -light field howitzer) carriers designated as '10.5cm

A large number of the captured French Char B tanks were converted into the flame-thrower model and saw action in Russia with the 223rd Panzer company.

General Heinz Guderian at the front commanding his troops during the massive encirclement battles of summer 1941.

leFH18/3(Sf) auf Geschutzwagen B-2(f)', also known as Sturmhaubitze B-2(f). This conversion was fairly simple and consisted of the removal of original turret armed with 47mm KwK 35(f) L/34 and replacement with a superstructure housing the howitzer. Along with the removal of turret, hull mounted gun was also removed and the opening covered with a bolted plate. The entire conversion was done by Rheinmetall-Borsig in Dusseldorf, and all of the resulting vehicles were issued to Sturmgeschütz Abteilung 200 stationed in France.

Some Chars were also converted to training tanks, designated as 'Panzerkampfwagen B-2(f) als Schulfahrzeug/Fahrschulwagen B2(f)'. According to original German captured tank inventories, as of July 1943 there were six B2(f) tanks as part of Army Group A (Eastern Front), 17 in the Balkans and 81 in the West. Chars were used for internal policing and security duties and remained in service as late as May 1945 in the Channel Islands. Some were recaptured by the French Resistance (e.g. FF1 -Forces Francaises de l'lnterieur - French Forces of the Interior) and used after the liberation of Paris.

The FCM Char de Rupture 2C (3C) was a heavy tank shaped by the lessons of the First World War and was the world's first multi-turreted tank, operated by a crew of 11 to 12 men. Only ten were manufactured from 1918 to 1921. In May 1940 six 3Cs were still operational but never reached the front line, due to a Luftwaffe Junkers Ju-87 Stuka dive bomber attack, which immobilised the train on which they were being carried and made unloading from their special railcars an impossible task. The abandoned tanks were then captured by the 8th Panzer Regiment of the 101 Panzer Division. The Germans designated 3Cs as Panzerkampfwagen 3C 74 1 (f) but none were used, and they were only evaluated in October 1940. Afterwards they were moved to the Renault Factory, where they were all probably scrapped in 1942.

CAPTURED BRITISH TANKS

Alongside the French army there was the British Expeditionary Force (BHF), 400,000 men strong with some 704 tanks of various types as of 10th May 1940.

The BEF began its evacuation from Dunkirk on 16th May 1940, which eventually evacuated some 340,000 allied soldiers but left behind all of its heavy equipment. Only 13 British tanks were brought back from France. The Germans captured all of the abandoned British tanks but

ARMOURED VEHICLE NOMENCLATURE

The Panzer tanks (Panzerkampfwagen) extensively used by Germany in World War II were initially abbreviated to 'PzKw', but the confusion this caused with the personnel carriers known by the abbreviation 'PzK' led to a change. Halfway through the war, armoured fighting vehicles consequently came to be appointed 'PzKpfw' or 'Pz.Kpfw'. A Roman numeral distinguished one vehicle type from another – and variants were identified by a capital-letter alphabetic Ausfuhrung number which was abbreviated to 'Ausf. Additionally, all special purpose vehicles of the Wehrmacht received a unique SdKfz number (Sonderkraftfahrzeug), which did not adjust from one version to the next. For example, all 12 versions of the PzKpfw III were known as Sd.Kfz 141. The number was only changed if an important variant was produced.

The final three German tanks of the war also received the names Tiger, Panther and Tiger II (also widely known as the King Tiger or Konigstiger). They became, for example. PzKpfw V Panther Ausf G. The designations of some tanks were converted retroactively, for example the PzKpfw VI Tiger Ausf H (SdKfz 181) was later re-designated as the PzKpfw VI Tiger I Ausf E. The Tiger II also lost its Roman-numeral type designator, becoming the PzKpfw Tiger II Ausf B (SdKfz 182). The Ausf designators were not always apportioned in alphabetical order. With the Tiger, the original Ausf letters - H and P -actually refer to the designers, Henschel and Porsche. Subvariants sometimes received an Arabic numeral after the alphabetic designator eg: PzKpfw IV Ausf F2. Tanks with type similarities but with different guns were set apart by a reference to its main weapon, either its nominal calibre, the length of its barrel or its own type designator. A PzKpfw III with the short-barrelled 7.5cm gun might be referred to as a PzKpfw III (75). Tigers were often distinguished from King Tigers by the identification of their main guns. The Tiger became PzKpfw VI (8.8cm KwK 36 L/56) and the King Tiger, PzKpfw VI (8.8cm KwK 43 L/71). In the assistance of further vehicle identification, unique sub-designators were used.

From 1938, prototype and experimental tanks first received a 'VK' designator standing for Volkettenkraftfahrzeug, a full-tracked motor vehicle. This was followed by four numbers, the first two describing its weight in tonnes, while the second two distinguished one prototype from another. When a similar specification was allocated to two or more manufacturers, a lettered abbreviation of their name was affixed in brackets e.g. VK 3001 (H) indicated a tank made by Henschel. From 1943 onwards, experimental tanks and those under development got a similar 'E' designation (for Entwicklungstyp, meaning development type) followed by an estimated weight-class.

This dramatic study shows German armour advancing past the blazing wrecks of Soviet tanks destroyed during the opening phase of Barbarossa.

only pressed around 250 into service due to their condition and a shortage of ammunition and spare parts. The majority were scrapped for parts to keep a Captured Panzer Company with three platoons equipped with British tanks into 1941.

The most numerous tank used by the BEF was the Vickers-Carden-Lloyd Light (Reconnaissance) Tank Mark VIB and VIC. Lightly armoured and armed, they were fast but unreliable and were of little or no combat value. Mark VIs were used by the Germans for training purposes by units stationed in France for the abortive Operation Seelowe (Sea Lion) - the invasion of England – while some equipped the 1st platoon of the Captured Panzer Company as of early 1940. In order to maintain the Mark VIs a number of damaged tanks were taken apart by repair workshops to provide spare parts.

The British Mark VIs became the first foreign vehicle to be converted into mobile artillery by Captain Alfred Becker. From June to December of 1940 Becker modified and converted 18 Mark VIs to self-propelled artillery. Conversion consisted of the installation of an armoured superstructure at the rear of the vehicle, which housed the main armament. Along with these conversions, four Mark VIs were converted to unarmed radio and observation tanks. This conversion was designated as Funk und Beobachtungspanzer auf Fahrgestell Mk. VI(e) - radio (an observation tank on Mark VI(e)'s chassis). Conversions were tested on the proving grounds at Beverlo in Belgium. In October 1941 the conversions were grouped in the 15th Artillery Battery of 227th Artillery Regiment of the 227th Infantry Division commanded by Becker, which was transferred to the Northern sector (Leningrad area) of the Eastern Front. In mid-1942 an additional 12 Mark VIs were converted to ammunition carriers designated as Munitionspanzer auf Fahrgestell Mk. VI(e).

The two-man Infantry Tank MU (All) Matilda I designated by the Germans as 'Infanterie Panzerkampfwagen MlU 747(e)' was reliable and well armoured, but it was also poorly armed and very slow. One hundred and thirty-nine Matilda Is were produced, 97 of which equipped two tank battalions of the BEF. The design was already obsolete by 1939 standards and the Germans made no use of any of captured Matilda Is, although it is possible that some had their turrets removed and used in the fortifications of the Atlantic Wall. Two examples were certainly tested at Kummersdorf in early 1941 but found wanting in almost every respect.

Of slightly more use was the four-man infantry tank Mark II (A 12), Matilda 11. This was supposedly an improved version of Matilda I, although in practice its design was completely different. The Matilda II was a very well armoured vehicle armed with a two-pounder (40mm) gun. Like the Matilda I, it was a slow but reliable vehicle. The BEF was equipped with 23 Matilda IIs and the Germans captured a few during the course of the campaign, including those abandoned and knocked out at Arras. Designated by the Germans as Infanterie Panzerkampfwagen Mk.ll 748(e). Two captured Matilda IIs were tested at Kummersdorf in early 1941 along with Matilda Is. A single Matilda II (turret number III) was used by the High Seas Instructional Command at Terneuzen in Holland for training purposes during the prelude to Operation Seelowe (Sealion). A Number of Matilda IIs had the turrets removed and the original guns were replaced by 50mm KwK 38 L/42 guns, which had formally equipped PzKpfw IIIs. The gun was protected by a large, wide shield; the vehicle also mounted two MG15 machine guns and anti-aircraft defence. Conversion was done by the High Seas Instructional Command workshop and was designated as '5cm KwK 1./42(M) auf Infanterie Panzerkampfwagen M II(e)' or as '5cm KwK auf Matilda(e)'. Once removed, the turrets were used in the fortifications of the Atlantic Wall.

The BEF had 57 Mark IV cruiser tanks, almost all of which were captured by the Germans, who designated them as 'Kreuzer Panzerkampfwagen Mk.lV 744(e)'. The Germans issued ten Mark IVs which were in service with the 2nd and 3rd platoon of the captured Panzer Company stationed in France in early 1941. Later on modified Mark IVs were transferred to Panzer Abteilung (Flamm) 100, which saw combat in the opening stage of the Operation Barbarossa in June and July 1941. Five tanks were scrapped for spare parts in order to keep those in service operational.

ENTER THE STURMGESCHÜTZ

One machine which had slipped quietly on to the battlefield during the French campaign was the Sturmgeschütz assault gun.

Under Blitzkrieg tactics, all of the tanks of the army were concentrated into the fast moving Panzer divisions, which would thrust deep into the rear positions of an enemy force, spreading panic and confusion as they advanced from the narrow point of penetration. As we have seen, the shock of the advance required a high level of artillery support at the point of attack, and also harnessed the extra power of air interdiction. But in the 1930s, the bulk of Germany's heavy artillery forces were still horse-drawn. What this meant was that the advancing tanks and motorised infantry would rapidly outstrip the artillery support.

Even mechanised prime movers like half-tracks had their disadvantages. The time taken to move into position and deploy the guns for action under battlefield conditions meant vital time was lost. In battle, split seconds literally meant the difference between life and death.

If artillery was to play a real role in the new mobile warfare it needed to be able to operate as close to the battle zone as possible, but the closer artillery pieces got to the action, the more vulnerable the gunners were to enemy fire. What was needed was an assault gun - a mobile artillery piece which could keep pace with the mechanised infantry, afford the gunners a measure of protection, and provide support on the battlefield at short notice, where it really mattered, in the very front line. A fully armoured and fully tracked mobile gun platform therefore had great appeal from the point of view of both mobility and crew protection. It also provided a means of providing close artillery support fire right in the very front line. Orders were despatched for prototype vehicles.

The successful prototype was produced in 1936 by the Alkett company. The final vehicle was actually constructed from two separate elements and it mounted a heavy 75mm gun on a Panzer III tank chassis. The 75mm was a heavier weapon than could normally be carried on a Panzer III, but the extra space for the gun was achieved by dispensing with the turret and setting the gun on a fixed mount with a limited traverse. The Sturmgeschütz was born.

Naturally, the Grenadiers fighting in the front line welcomed this development with open arms. Here was an artillery piece which could fight with the infantry at the crucial point of the battlefield and keep pace with the lightning advances of the Blitzkrieg era.

Throughout the long years of the Second World War the Sturmgeschütz crews never came

The Sturmgeschütze viewed from the enemy point of view. This propaganda photograph was probably taken in Russia during 1942.

A war artist provides a vivid impression of the cooperation between the Panzer grenadiers and the Sturmgeschütze.

to regard themselves as tank men. They wore different uniforms, and considered themselves to be artillery men who happened to man mobile assault guns – but they were still gunners at heart.

From the gunner's point of view, they quickly grew to love the Sturmgeschütz. After all, they were now protected against direct infantry fire and felt themselves impervious to anything but direct artillery fire. The powerful 75mm gun meant they packed a real punch in the attack.

The Sturmgeschütz had a crew of four: the commander, driver, loader and gunner. It soon became the proud boast of the Sturmgeschütz crews that their men were all volunteers, always ready to answer the infantryman's call to 'bring up the guns.' The new assault gunners took to the role with great enthusiasm. Although the cramped interior of each Geschutze officially had room for only 44 rounds, the crews soon found that they could carry 90 rounds of ammunition by stacking extra rounds in layers on the floor of the vehicle. This meant the guns could stay in action and continue to give their support to the infantry for longer periods. In the coming years that would be a great advantage.

Despite the early signs of promise, these first machines were produced in small numbers and only 30 Geschutze were available for the French campaign of 1940. But they acquitted themselves well in their first actions. Orders were immediately given for the production of a further 500 machines. These machines equipped the first Sturmgeschütze batteries which served in the Blitzkrieg campaigns, through the Balkans and into Russia.

Initially, the Sturmgeschütze were organised into independent battalions. Each battalion was composed of three troops, which originally had six guns each. The commander of the battalion also had his own vehicle. In later years the number of vehicles in each troop was raised to ten and the battalions were renamed as Brigades which, in theory, fielded 31 Sturmgeschütz. In practice, these ideals were hardly ever achieved and only highly favoured formations received the full compliment.

In battle these independent brigades were allocated to support infantry formations for a specific action and came under the command of these formations. As the war developed the Sturmgeschütz commanders naturally gained a wealth of battle experience through almost constant exposure to action. In practice it was frequently the infantry commanders who took the lead from the more experienced assault gun leaders.

The official regulations stressed that the Sturmgeschütz should be employed en masse. But the constant demands of a terrible war meant that they were more often employed as single battalions or even single machines.

One shortcoming of the early Sturmgeschütz models was the lack of a machine gun for close support against enemy infantry. This was rectified in 1941 with the introduction of the machine gun mounted on the Model E, of which a further 272 were produced.

WITTMANN MOVES TO THE STURMGESCHÜTZ

Among those who would see action in the assault was Michael Wittmann. Wittmann, together with several other NCOs and men, had now transferred to Juterbog, where the self-propelled assault battery was being formed. There, he and his colleagues traded in their black Panzer uniforms for grey assault gun tunics. It was to be two years before he would see Panzer black again. This was the start of Wittmann's association with armoured fighting vehicles which was to lead him to fame and infamy throughout the civilised world. There was much to learn. As we have seen, the assault guns were armed with the short-barrelled 75mm gun, which had little in common with the feeble 20mm cannon carried by the armoured cars, but Wittmann soon showed exceptional promise with the new weapon. After training, the fledgling assault gun battery was sent to garrison duty in France.

THE ALLIED VIEW

The Sturmgeschütz was to become such a fixed part of the thinking of the German forces that, five years after the French campaign, the US army handbook dedicated an extended section to the German use and handling of assault guns:

"The assault guns are organised in assault gun battalions and are under the control of the division commander.

The Germans regard their self-propelled assault guns as decisive weapons to be employed, particularly at the point of main effort. In cooperation with infantry they facilitate the penetration and breakthrough. These weapons, the Germans believe, complement artillery fire by their ability to follow the infantry right up to an objective.. Their use for small actions before an attack is forbidden so as not to betray their presence. Surprise is sought by bringing them into position by night and camouflaging their assembly area. Used primarily to neutralise enemy support weapons at short ranges over open sights, assault guns are preferably employed in concentrations; to employ them singly or in comparatively small numbers is frowned upon by the Germans.

German assault guns advance with or just behind the infantry: they never go ahead of the infantry. When an objective reached, the assault guns do not remain with the infantry while the position is being consolidated but retire about 1000 yards to await further assignment.

In close combat the assault guns are rather helpless and therefore it is the task of the infantry to keep the enemy away from the assault guns;

Newly-organised assault-gun escort batteries have the same task."

A DANGEROUS DEVELOPMENT

In early 1941 there was a further significant but ominous development. Hitler sought to rapidly expand the number of Panzer Divisions from the existing ten to a new level of 20. However, there was clearly insufficient manufacturing capacity to create the new machines, or the time to

A demonstration of the building of the Sturmgeschütze and Panzer IIIs which appeared in the pages of Signal magazine.

An artist's impression from the pages of Signal magazine illustrating the difficulties of moving vehicles under combat conditions. In this evocative image, a Sturmegeschze of the late war variety is being used to pull another machine out of trouble under fire.

recruit and train the hundreds of thousands of men who would be needed. With a typical rash flourish Hitler solved the problem at a stroke by reducing the number of regiments in a Panzer Division from two to one. He then used the extra regiments to form the tank elements of ten new Panzer Divisions. Although this exercise effectively doubled the number of Divisions in a short space of time it did so by reducing the tank strength of the Divisions from the 1940 level of over three hundred machines, to the new 1941 level of around one hundred and fifty. This dramatic reduction in fighting strength was to have dire consequences later in the war when breakdowns and casualties would frequently mean that a Panzer Division which could field 80 machines was in good shape.

OPERATION MARITA

In August 1940 German divisions began transferring to the occupied areas of Poland in order to reinforce the attenuated frontier defences. For the rest of the year the build up on the eastern front continued unabated. During this period the German forces in Poland were frequently regrouped to conceal their numbers. Before the storm could be unleashed there was another matter to be taken care of.

With the new year there arose an unexpected opportunity for the Blitzkrieg forces to test their expertise once more. Mussolini launched an ill-advised, ill-fated campaign in Greece, which left Italian forces floundering. Early in 1941 he turned to his ally Hitler for help.

Realising that their success in repelling the Italians was likely to bring German vengeance down upon them, the Greeks appealed to their British allies for aid. The reinforcements sent by Britain proved woefully inadequate. A declaration of war against Yugoslavia and Greece simultaneously was the signal that Blitzkrieg was about to be unleashed again. It burst over Yugoslavia on 6th April.

The same day Belgrade was heavily bombed and the Germans tore through the country. Zagreb, Sarajevo and Skopje fell in quick succession and just 12 days later Yugoslavia was occupied. Greece was now the front line.

After the short burst of activity which had characterised the lightning campaign through France, the long of barracks duty hung heavy on Wittmann, who was keen to see action again. He was not to get his wish until 6 April 1941, when the Balkans Campaign began. The German forces advanced through Yugoslavia to Greece where, in addition to Greek forces, their opponents included English and Commonwealth troops. Wittmann's assault gun was involved in the fierce fighting for the Klidi Pass, which fell only after heavy resistance. Next, the Liebstandarte had to fight its way through the Klisswa Pass and on to Corinth and Olympia against fierce opposition from the Greek army. The fighting in Greece ended on 30 April 1941. After pausing to rest in Thessalia in May the Liebstandarte was sent through Yugoslavia to Camp Dieditz near Wischau, where they awaited the next phase of the war - the invasion of Russia.

Two German Corps had stormed into northern Greece from Bulgaria on the 6th April, followed on the 8th by the 2nd Panzer Division. Blitzkrieg was once again proving to be unstoppable as the invading armies drove towards the south with the British retreating before them. On the 19th the British forces had been overwhelmed and evacuated to Crete.

They were hardly given time to draw breath.

On 20th May the skies over Crete were suddenly filled with the German aircraft of Operation Merkur.

A relentless bombing raid on the island was the prelude to the first major airborne assault in history. An awesome sight met the eyes of the defenders as the departing aircraft left a cascade of parachutes behind them and the 7th Fliegerdivision dropped earthwards. What followed was due to the greatest failure of German intelligence up to that point in the war. The British were ready for the paratroopers and 50 percent of them were dead before they reached the ground.

The carnage was no help to the British, and was almost an irrelevance in the great Blitzkrieg push. Eight days later the British were being evacuated once more and Germany seemed invincible.

The succession of victories was unbroken and thus far German casualties overall had been comparatively small, so that the nation had scarcely felt itself to be at war. People were still full of wonder and admiration. Only a handful of the highest commanders were privy to the extraordinary cataclysm which was to come.

CAPTURED BRITISH ARMOUR

The fall of Greece meant that the total 300 vehicles used by the British and Commonwealth Forces were captured by the Germans in Yugoslavia and Greece during Operation Marita. The Yugoslavian 1st Tank Battalion (Batalion Bornih Kola) also yielded some 110 tanks.

Captured Yugoslavian and Greek tanks along with tanks transferred from France were assigned to infantry divisions in Serbia, Croatia and eventually Bosnia. A number were also used for railway defence in those areas and in armoured trains.

Captured from the British were some 140 tanks, including Matilda II, Cruiser (e.g. Mark II) and Light Tanks, hut it is unknown how many were pressed, if any at all, into German service.

A French tank crew is taken into captivity. The prisoners are immobilised by the simple expedient of forcing them to drop their trousers to their ankles.

ESTIMATED GERMAN ARMOURED VEHICLE PRODUCTION 1933-1945

Tanks	1933-1938	1939	1940	1941	1942	1943	1944	1945	Totals
Panzer I	1,000	500	-	-	-	-	-	-	1,500
Panzer II	800	700	200	200	100	-	-	-	2,000
Panzer III	100	200	1,400	1,600	1,800	400	-	-	5,500
Panzer IV	200	200	1,000	1,200	2,000	2,000	1,700	300	8,600
Panzer V	-	-	-	-	-	2,000	4,500	300	6,800
Panzer VI	-	-	-	-	-	650	630	-	1,280
Panzer VI (B)	-	-	-	-	-	-	377	107	484
Total	2,100	1,600	2,600	3,000	3,900	5,050	7,207	707	26,164

Tank Destroyers	1933-1938	1939	1940	1941	1942	1943	1944	1945	Totals
PzJag I	-	-	100	100	-	-	-	-	200
Stug III/IV	-	-	40	500	1,000	3,000	5,000	700	10,240
Marder II	-	-	-	-	200	350	-	-	550
Marder III	-	-	-	-	280	400	500	-	1,180
Elefant	-	-	-	-	-	88	-	-	88
Hertzer	-	-	-	-	-	-	2,000	500	2,500
Nashorn	-	-	-	-	-	200	300	-	500
PzJag IV	-	-	-	-	-	700	1,000	300	2,000
Jagd Panther	-	-	-	-	-	-	350	32	382
Jagd Tiger	-	-	-	-	-	-	50	30	80
Brummbär	-	-	-	-	-	200	100	-	300
Sturmtiger	-	-	-	-	-	-	20	-	20
Wespe	-	-	-	-	-	400	270	-	670
Hummel	-	-	-	-	-	-	560	100	660
Total	0	0	140	600	1,480	5,338	10,150	1,662	19,370

THE WESTERN DESERT 1941-1942

"It is essential that the forces fighting under my command in this theatre are properly supplied with adequate stocks ammunition and fuel. These are the life blood of the Panzer forces."

ERWIN ROMMEL, 1942

The fighting in the desert began with Italy's entry into the war in 1940. British forces stationed in Egypt and Sudan were confronted by much larger Italian forces on two adjoining fronts, but the British enjoyed certain advantages.

As a result of their superior training, the smaller British forces took the fight to the Italians, and appeared from nowhere with aggressive tactics, which soon won the day.

On 9th December two squadrons of Matildas under the command of General O'Connor successfully used the element of surprise and attacked a strong Italian position at Sidi Barrani without the customary opening artillery barrage. By 10.00am the fort was captured, every Italian tank was knocked out and the British had 2,000 prisoners to contend with.

'Operation Compass' followed, an astonishing 500-mile drive westwards during which ten Italian divisions were effectively destroyed, with the capture of hundreds of tanks and guns.

Casualties amongst O'Connor's men came to less than 2,000 whereas the Italians sustained losses of 100,000 dead or wounded and a further 130,000 taken prisoner. Had the Italians not escorted themselves to prison camps the logistics of dealing with so many captives would have presented major difficulties.

A Panzer III negotiates the rudimentary roads of North Africa. The find sand and dust thrown up by the tanks had a disastrous effect on the engines and running gear.

DIFFICULT CONDITIONS

The early battles were fought using some very humble machines. The North African desert campaign was, in many respects, the ideal battlefield for tanks. But the desert was to prove a harsh mistress offering the tantalising promise of success only to withdraw its promise just at the point where victory seemed within reach. In turn, the Italians, then the British and Germans, and finally the Americans, would each experience the thrill of conquest followed by an unexpected defeat. The first to experience the roller-coaster ride of the ebbs and flows of tank warfare in the desert were the Italians.

Italian tanks were no match for the British tanks and tactics, and in consequence the British Army enjoyed great success against the Italians. In particular, the Italian light tanks were so ineffective as to prove almost comical. But even the British medium tanks had their limitations.

In contrast to the Italian tanks, the British Matilda tank was very slow, but effective. It was the Matilda's ability to absorb punishment that earned it the nickname 'Queen of the battlefield'. The unmistakable squat shape of the Matilda fought throughout the desert campaign. Many captured Matildas were even used by the Germans against their former owners.

While the Matilda took on the job of supporting the infantry, the armoured punch of the British tank brigade was provided by the Crusader tanks. It was their job to engage enemy tanks.

By February 1941 O'Connor was eagerly preparing to advance on Tripoli to eliminate Axis forces in Africa completely, but Churchill decided that O'Connor's battle-hardened divisions should be dispatched urgently to Greece.

The British success was so swift and comprehensive that the campaign was nearly over when Hitler at last decided to help his Italian Allies. German forces entered the campaign in February 1941 and their tactics, leadership and superior weaponry immediately changed the status quo in the desert.

The Afrika Korps typified all that was innovative in the German war machine. In its brief history, of just two years and three months, the Afrika Korps stung the allied forces into a massive war of attrition and won for itself an honourable mention in the annals of military history.

The deadly '88' in action during the early stages of the North African campaign. These guns were to prove the most feared anti-tank weapons of the war.

In 1940 the Wehrmacht was singularly ill-equipped for battle beneath the relentless sun of North Africa. German military formations were created for European conditions. They did not possess even one unit specifically trained for fighting in desert conditions. By contrast the British had years of desert experience dating back to before the First World War. In fact, the British had been active in North Africa since the days of Napoleon and maintained a permanent presence in Egypt.

Desperate to keep his Axis partner in the war, in January 1941 Hitler signed Führer Directive Number 22, code-named Operation Sonnenblume, or sunflower. It authorised the transport of a small German force to Tripoli to assist the Italians in blocking further British advances.

On February 14th units of Germany's newly created Afrika Korps began to land in Tripoli. These new arrivals were already seasoned warriors and they brought with them impressive modern weaponry. They were commanded by one of Germany's most able and imaginative practitioners of tank warfare. General Erwin Rommel. Rommel was an aggressive commander who exploited any weaknesses in his enemy to the full. With a series of brilliantly executed battle plans Rommel earned the title 'The Desert Fox'. He was held in awe by his enemies.

The Matilda and the obsolete A9 Cruiser tanks now had to face German machines with better armaments, better armour and better speed and range. The British now had to contend with the Panzer II, Ill and IV.

The Afrika Korps was, as its name suggested, only a corps in size, but it was a relatively small corps with only two Panzer Divisions. The second 'Panzer Division' did not even arrive until May 1941. In reality the first unit was a light division, (the 5th light division).

The Desert War has often been described as the last example of a chivalrous war; nevertheless, it was a hard-fought affair.

By a series of lightning armoured reconnaissance probes, Rommel quickly established that the strength of the allied forces ranged against him had been overestimated. He was faced by the Second Army division, newly arrived from Britain, and not yet acclimatised to desert conditions. The second British armoured division consisted of one weakened armoured brigade already short of transport and with worn-out tanks. They were supported by a similarly weakened 9th Australian Division. A third British formation was held in reserve in Tobruk. These forces were under the command of General Wavell.

Wavell had been siphoning off forces for Crete and then Greece since January 1941, so when the Afrika Korps finally struck in March 1941 there was a very, very thin screen facing Rommel and his new force.

The British who had swept the Italians back were now at the end of an enormously long logistical chain; essentially, they could not support, from Egypt, the number of troops who were now in the far western desert.

The Germans had trained and developed the ideas of mobile and manoeuvrable warfare to a fine pitch during the Polish and French Campaigns which meant that the Afrika Korps was a well balanced armed force, able to traverse almost any terrain and fight almost any opponent.

As Rommel began his attacks in Cyrenaica it became abundantly clear he possessed an advantage in the quality of his weaponry. Against the British total of 22 cruiser and 25 light tanks, the 5th Panzer Regiment fielded 150 tanks - and nearly half of those were the superior Mark III and IVs. In addition, Rommel already possessed a few 88mm anti-aircraft guns, which he would use to such devastating effect as his principal anti-tank gun.

Where the British tended to use their tanks independently of their other arms, the Germans developed a very close coordination between their tanks and tank artillery and infantry. This made them a much tougher proposition in the desert battles.

Vital to Rommel's tactical success was his continued use of the bait technique, where his tanks would first attempt the allied tanks with a frontal probe. When the allied tanks then charged towards the Panzers, the German tanks would fall back behind their screen of 88mm guns which, with a greater range, could then open up with decisive killing shots on the advancing armour. This was a technique he used again and again, and it was something the British never seemed to be able to counter.

THE DESERT THEATRE

The desert in North Africa has been described as a tactician's paradise and a quartermaster's hell. For a progressive thinker like Rommel it was a paradise because of its vast, uninhabited emptiness, with no changing seasons, no partisans, no resistance groups and no urban centres to slow the movements of armoured divisions. But for the men in charge off logistical support it was a pure hell because everything – fuel, ammunition, food and weapons - had to pass along tortuously extended lines of supply which became ever more Stretched as the Afrika Korps stormed eastwards.

All of the supplies for Rommel's army in terms of ammunition, petrol, food and so on had to be transported from Italy. The Italian merchant ships had to run the gauntlet, posed by the British island of Malta, with its submarines and shore-based aircraft. Although Rommel's by-line was relatively short, a matter of a mere 60 miles, it was actually very vulnerable to British interdiction. The supplies then had to be transported over land on the one road in North Africa, the Via Balboa, built by the Italians. As Rommel's army advanced eastwards his supply line stretched; once Rommel reached El Alamein, only 60 miles from Alexandria, his supply line was 1,300 miles long, all the way from Tripoli.

One of the great problems of operating over those great distances was that the trucks themselves used fuel. It has been estimated that somewhere between ten and fifteen per cent of all the fuel that the Afrika Korps needed was actually spent in sustaining vehicles for the supply route. In those conditions, over very rough roads, vehicle breakdowns were inevitable. At any one time up to about thirty per cent of Rommel's vehicles were actually in for repair. The British helped him enormously and they seemed to abandon their tanks with careless regularity. Indeed, by the summer of 1942 virtually all of the Afrika Korps transport was composed of British trucks.

Like the Allies before them the Afrika Korps soon realised there were geographical limitations which would force them to operate within a band stretching approximately fifty miles south from the Mediterranean coast; further south than that lay the limitless sand dunes with deep desert, impassable to wheeled or tracked vehicles alike.

Within that 50-mile passable band of terrain the one road, the Via Balboa, skirted the coast, and along this tarmac artery ran Rommel's armoured units and his columns of supply lorries. Petrol was one of the most precious commodities. From the outset it was always rationed and any unauthorised use of a vehicle was heavily punished.

A WAR OF ATTRITION

Now, balanced tank forces, backed with artillery, fought each other head on in what ultimately was to became a war of attrition. The objective was to knock out the other side's tanks, deny the enemy the battlefield so he couldn't recover and repair losses. At the same time it was necessary to attack his supply routes and bases, making difficult the maintenance of his mechanised forces.

Tanks of each side took a fearsome toll on each other and, contrary to popular belief, British tanks gave as good as they got. In the early months of the campaign the British in fact had the advantage in the ever-changing balance between armour and armament.

Initially the German Panzer III had only 30mm of frontal armour and the Panzer IV had even less, at 20mm; both of these machines could easily be pierced by British anti-tank weapons. In contrast the early Crusaders enjoyed 40mm whilst the redoubtable Matildas had 80mm of frontal armour. The 50mm gun of the Panzer III could not pierce the armour of the Crusader except on the side, while the Matilda could not be penetrated even at ranges as close as 500 yards.

Despite the limitations of his armour, Rommel's conduct of battle was bold and resourceful. In Panzer attacks the tanks would be used as a wedge - the 'Panzerkeil' - closely supported by other services; artillery to soften the objective, pioneers to deal with obstacles, infantry to take and hold ground, and of course the Stukas to act as supplementary artillery. Rommel led from the front and specialised in the concentration of a superior force against a single point. As the other great

A peaceful study of a Panzer II on the shores of the Libyan coast. The crewman is in the process of spreading out an air recognition flag on the rear deck.

exponent of German tank warfare, Heinz Guderian, was fond of saying: "Kotzen, nicht kleckern". In other words "Spew, don't dribble." Rommel certainly took the message to heart.

The North Africa terrain was particularly harsh. Although one might tend to think of great swathes of sand dunes, in actual fact much of the terrain was very stony barren desert, and this look an enormous toll not just on the men, but on the vehicles too. Tank tracks were particularly susceptible to damage. The sand blown up by the constant movement of vehicles meant that the engine air filters suffered much greater wear and tear, and the quantity of lubricants needed to keep the engines running properly and the amount of maintenance was vastly increased.

Initially, the Panzers had arrived with normal European air filters fitted to the engines. Inevitably, the sand penetrated through these filters and the cylinder walls of the engines could be scoured to a standstill within 800 or 1,000 miles.

Together, the German and Italian forces in North Africa needed at least seventy thousand tons of supplies every month. All of it had to come by sea from ports in southern Italy, and all of it came under attack by the Royal Navy and the Royal Air Force. Minor amounts of supplies were flown in from time to time, but the unarmed Junkers 52 transport aircraft were rarely available in sufficient numbers and, in any case, they presented themselves as easy targets for any marauding RAF fighters.

The logistical difficulties faced by the Afrika Korps were enormous, and there is no question that they were usually chronically short of supplies. It is nonetheless interesting to look at the statistics for the amount of equipment which was shipped from Italy; the figures would appear to suggest that well over 90 per cent of the men, vehicles and supplies which were dispatched actually reached the Afrika Korps. Clearly there was a regular channel of supply, and it was not quite as bleak a picture as is often painted.

Rommel was eager to advance as far and as quickly as possible. He had his eyes focussed on the Suez Canal, his final objective. Frequently his supply lines were stretched to breaking point - but he was a man indifferent to such limitations. Despite the fact it was over eight hundred miles from his main supply port in Tripoli to the Egyptian frontier, Rommel viewed that as a logistical matter for the High Command to solve, whereas it was his job to fight the war on the ground.

Every German tank was fitted with wireless and had tremendous flexibility of response in a changing battle situation. The Germans were also far ahead in the techniques of anti-tank warfare. By 1941 the 37mm anti-tank gun had been replaced with the larger 50mm Pak 38. The Germans also frequently employed the famous 88mm anti-aircraft gun in the anti-tank role. This gun could even take out the sturdy Malilda at ranges of up to two thousand yards. Placed defensively, Rommel could use a screen of 88mm guns to knock out British tanks before the Panzers were even engaged. This innovative use of weapons substantially reduced the advantages which came from superior numbers of British tanks.

The harsh brilliance of the desert sun imposed its own rules on the conduct of the North African campaign, with the men suffering an almost daily form of desert blindness. It was soon established that between dawn and 9am and again between 4pm and dusk a man could accurately identify friend or enemy vehicle at anything between two and five thousand yards. In the shimmering heat of full sun that accurate range dropped to 1,500 yards.

Rommel was very much a hands-on commander who always wanted to know what was happening at the sharp end. He believed that he had to have what he called a finger-tip feel for the battlefield so that he could be there in person during the crisis of a battle. This meant that Rommel was often able to react much faster to events than his British counterparts who relied upon the standard chain of command. The downside meant that Rommel left his chief of staff and headquarters often miles behind as he toured the battlefield in his personal half-track.

Rommel did have a very good radio communication system, but this was often jammed by the British, and in consequence his commanders often did not know where their Korps Commander (and later their Army Commander) actually was.

In the featureless desert the art of camouflage was another skill quickly learned by the men of the Afrika Korps. When the first Panzer Mark IIs, IIIs and IVs arrived they were painted in the Wehrmacht colours of grey green - far too highly visible in the desert. In the absence of desert colour paint those first tanks were sprayed with oil and then hot sand thrown over them until they more or less blended in with the background. The crews quickly learned to make skilful use of netting and the camel thorn bush to break up the outline of their vehicles.

As the war progressed the calibre and power of anti-tank guns increased from the relatively weak 37mm gun to the awesome power of the high velocity 88mm. The '88' was originally designed as an anti-aircraft gun, which needed to generate enormous power to fire a heavy shell 20,000 feet into the air.

When the German infantry discovered that this powerful gun could also be used to fire over a flat trajectory against tanks, a devastating new weapon was born. The massive velocity of its armour piercing shells spelt death for thousands of Russian and allied tanks during the years from 1939 to 1945

Throughout the war the '88' was the most feared adversary for all of the tank men in the allied armies. The only drawback of this weapon was that it was very cumbersome and needed to be towed into action, but once it was deployed in concealed and camouflaged positions it was a deadly menace.

Mounted on towed trailers, the 88mm gun could be swiftly deployed and engage the enemy at 2,000 yards range - long before the allied tank guns were close enough to reply. The 88mm had one more advantage - besides the armour piercing range, it also fired high explosive shells. The Panzer Mark III and IV

Rommel in Africa from the May 1941 issue of Signal magazine. At this time Rommel was enjoying the first fruits of success as an armoured leader and shows little sign of the enormous fatigue which would go on to characterise later pictures.

94

tanks could also fire high explosive shells which were devastating against infantry, but had little effect against the British tanks, such as the Crusader and Valentine.

Despite the fact that he personally had to cross large areas of featureless terrain, the restless energy of Rommel drove his men forward. When he was not at the helm of his command car, 'Greiff, Rommel was to be found reconnoitring the ground from the cockpit of his Feisler Storch reconnaissance aircraft, from which he was constantly urging his troops forward. Encouraged and exhorted by the gadfly energy of their commanding officer, the tank crews surged forward.

Behind Rommel's early successes in his advance eastwards was his firm belief that he could crush the allied forces and continue his advance all the way to Alexandria and the Suez canal. From there, he could set his sights on the Caucasus in the southern Soviet Union where he hoped to achieve a classic pincer movement - sinking a decisive blow in Germany's war.

THE GERMAN ADVANTAGE

A major difficulty experienced by the British tanks in the desert was the lack of a dual-purpose gun, one which could fire high explosives as well as armour piercing shells. The two-pounder anti-tank guns which were standard in British tanks could not fire the effective high explosive shells which were required to deal with anti-tank guns and infantry on the battlefield.

This problem had actually been foreseen prior to the Second World War and the interim solution was to provide two close-support tanks for each squadron, fitted with 3in Howitzer. Used mainly as a means of laying smoke screens, the close support tanks carried few high explosive shells on board. Generally, the Crusader was used in this role.

In the desert the battlefield was now dominated by the tanks; infantry were helpless without armoured support. The balance of power between the allied and axis forces was now measured by who could field the most tanks. Keeping these tanks in the held was another matter altogether. They required intensive servicing and repair. The harshness of the desert exacerbated this problem, and the supply line organisation assumed vital importance in bringing forward fuel, ammunition and spare parts. This over-extended supply line also dealt with the recovery of tanks from the battlefield, replacement vehicles and all of the myriad requirements for an army in the field. Attacking supply lines on land, sea or air became of crucial importance to both sides.

Not all tank knocked out by enemy fire were actually destroyed. Often, they were brought in to be repaired; those not immediately repairable provided much needed spares for others. At the same time the enemy had to be denied the opportunity to use the battlefield losses in this way. Repaired enemy vehicles could be pressed into service against their original owners, and enemy equipment salvaged from the battlefield provided intelligence on the latest vehicles, armour, weapons and ammunition. The recovery mechanics and tank transporter drivers of both sides often plied their trade under fire.

Unloading the tanks of the Afrika Korps in Tripoli during May 1941. The allied interdiction campaign, although severe, was not as all-embracing as many sources would appear to suggest. More than 90% of the armoured vehicles dispatched to Rommel actually arrived safely in Tripoli.

For example, at the Halfaya Pass battles the British lost 91 tanks, which included 64 Matildas. A considerable number of these losses were due to mechanical breakdowns, but a combination of time and shortage of transporters meant most ended up being left on the battlefield. In this instance the Germans were able to utilise the captured vehicles, Rommel himself acquiring a British armoured command truck, which he named 'Mammoth'.

VEHICLE RECOVERY

As Rommel's tenuous supply line grew even more difficult to maintain, it became essential to recover as many damaged or broken down vehicles as possible. While this was also a factor in British thinking, it was a less pressing issue as the Eighth Army was comparatively well served with replacements. Control of the field after the battle was vital for Rommel. It allowed the Afrika Korps to salvage allied and enemy machines alike.

Most vehicle casualties were recoverable. Obviously if a shell is blasted through the middle of a tank it usually made a wreck of the inside, but a more common type of tank casualty would be a missing track link, damaged tracks or damaged suspensions.

Despite the fact that in February 1941 only elements of the 5th (Light) Division had arrived, Rommel wasted no time. Within ten days he launched his first assault. Without waiting for his full force to be assembled he moved swiftly against the inactive forward British units, throwing them back in confusion. The British were dismayed to see shells from their two-pounder guns merely bouncing off the German armour.

The follow-up was immediate, and in early April the British were forced to evacuate Benghazi. O'Connor, hastily recalled from leave, was captured. The momentum of Rommel's brilliant offensive did not falter. Within a few months, in a spectacular change of fortunes, all of O'Connor's gains were reversed and the Afrika Korps successfully laid siege to the port stronghold of Tobruk.

During 1941 the real weakness of German tank design was still not discovered. Several false conclusions were drawn from the conquest of the Balkans and Greece. These easy victories supported the continued German belief that their tanks were the best in the world. Although the design work that was to lead to the Tiger had begun, there was little real urgency.

Up to the summer of 1941, Germany's main adversary had been Britain, and British tank design lagged behind Germany's. In the North African campaign the poor performance of the British Crusader tanks only gave fresh support to the German view that the Panzer IIIs and IVs were at least equal to anything the Allies could throw at them. The Crusader was particularly badly designed and it was plagued by a host of mechanical failures. Eventually, the British army lost faith in their own tanks altogether and in 1943 when the victorious British and American forces embarked from Africa for the invasion of Italy, all of the British tanks were left behind.

Despite the limitations of the British machines, there were signs of dangerous flaws in Germany's tank capability. In the relative backwater of the desert war, even the unspectacular British Matilda tank was considered a success against the Italian forces and frequently held its own against the Germans. The gun on the Matilda, which was typical of most tanks of his period, was the two-pounder, a 40mm weapon, but it only fired solid shot. In other words, it was only any use firing against enemy tanks. This was fine as far as it went, but once the Germans came to the desert and started mixing tanks and anti-tank guns in the attack, a dual-purpose gun was needed, something which not only fired solid armour piercing shot to take out enemy tanks, but which could also fire high explosive shells. The advantage of this was seen when the American tanks arrived, notably the General Grant.

Once again, superior German battlefield tactics were overcoming the limitations of her armoured forces. But these successes also reinforced a leisurely attitude towards the development of new types. By 1941 the evolution of German tank design was proceeding much too slowly, and it was to have deadly consequences from which Germany would never recover. The shock was to be delivered in Russia.

In the late autumn General Auchinleck organised another offensive in the desert. For a while it enjoyed a measure of success and in December Benghazi was recaptured, but it fell again to the Germans as early in 1942. Rommel once more began to drive eastwards. Egypt itself was menaced.

After his success against the British counter-offensive, 'Operation Battleaxe'. Rommel wrote to his wife, Lucy: 'I have been three days on the road going round the battlefield. The joy of my troops is tremendous.' One of his staff officers remarked:

'He is already in the process of becoming a hero'. And he was a hero and a legend, worshipped by his men, respected by his enemies.

By this time, however, the German supply lines were uncomfortably over-extended and the number of operational tanks was depleted by such a long and arduous advance. Auchinleck decided to make a stand at El Alamein, where large salt marshes inland prevented Rommel out-flanking the British to the south. Throughout July Rommel's weakened vanguard made repeated forays against the British positions around El Alamein, but each assault was successfully beaten back. Even so, the British 8th Army remained alarmingly vulnerable.

Rommel, now created a Field Marshall following the dramatic capture of Tobruk, tried to break through the El Alamein defences and planned to use captured fuel to thrust onwards to Cairo. His first priority was to consolidate and replenish his forces. Despite receiving only limited supplies and reinforcements, by the end of August Rommel felt able to resume his offensive.

The same period saw notable changes in the British command structure. In August 1942 General Sir Bernard Montgomery took over as commander of the British Eighth Army. He was to reap the benefit of the new equipment and reinforcements pouring into the desert campaign. But Monty (as he was known to his troops) was a different breed of commander; he had taken the lessons of the First World War and the opening phase of victory in the Second World War in France to heart. He talked to his men, was seen by them, and gave them a victory at Alam el Halfa.

He realised there was one vital ridge at Alam el Halfa which Rommel must try to take. Accordingly he prepared a defence in depth. British code breakers had deciphered the enemy signals and German convoys from Italy were regularly destroyed in the Mediterranean. Montgomery also knew when Rommel intended to strike. When it came, the battle of Alam el Halfa was brief. A deep belt of mines impeded the initial German advance and when the main offensive began the following morning the 200 German and 240 Italian tanks came under punishing bombing attacks. Rommel had achieved neither surprise nor speed and by the first week of September the Afrika Korps was back where it started.

In 1942 there was more good news for the British. The American M3 medium tank, known to the British as the 'Grant' was introduced into the campaign and first used at Gazala. The Grant mounted two tank guns to provide the solution to the need for a gun to fire high explosive and armour piercing shells. The 75mm howitzer was placed in a sponson on the right hand side of the tank - a welcome upgrading of firepower. At last the British tank forces had a good high explosive capability which could be used against German anti-tank guns and their crews. The other gun on the Grant was the anti-tank weapon, mounted in an alarmingly lofty turret perched on top of

the tank, which produced a dangerously high silhouette. This height made it difficult for the Grant to adopt a hull-down position (where a tank hides its body behind cover, leaving the turret exposed, thus reducing its target area to the enemy). The two guns meant that the Grant needed a crew of six, a large number for a tank. Five hundred Grants were sent to the Middle East.

But Grant was very much an interim solution. The most important American tank to enter the North African Campaign was the M4A1 medium tank, the Sherman. Shermans

An excellent study of a Panzer II on active service with the Afrika Korps. The 2cm gun was an improvement on the machine-gun armed Panzer I but by 1941 the Panzer II had long been eclipsed as a battle tank.

first appeared in action at El Alamein in November 1942. This tank would eventually become the mainstay of the allies on all battlefields. It was not a particularly heavily armoured tank but its real strength was derived from the sheer quantity manufactured. In a war of attrition the US manufacturing muscle would beat German technical superiority. The Sherman suffered the terrible attribute of bursting into flames even when hit by a non-explosive anti-tank shell. This led to it being given the nickname of the 'Ronson' because as the soldiers quipped with macabre humour, it 'lights first time'. The German nickname was equally cruel: they christened it the 'Tommycooker'! Despite its limitations, the volume of Shermans on the battlefield ultimately proved to be a deciding factor.

However, the US was not the only producer of new tanks in 1942. The British had introduced the A22, named the Churchill. This tank first appeared in March 1942 armed with the standard British two-pounder gun; the Mark III and IV variants were up-gunned to a six-pounder (57mm) gun. The Churchill, weighing in at nearly 40 tons, was powered by a 350bhp Bedford engine. Although it was a slow, ponderous tank reaching only 18mph on a good day, its frontal armour was a massive 102mm, which gave a great deal of comfort to the five-man crew. Three Churchills took part in the Battle of El Alamein for evaluation purposes. They passed the test and the British 21st Army Tank Brigade, which arrived in North Africa in March 1943, was fully equipped with Churchills.

The tank strength of the Eighth Army had by August 1942 reached 935 machines, with an effective strength of tanks fit for action of 762 machines. The numbers game was running against the Germans; Rommel could by now field only 200 tanks, but their qualitative situation had improved. A hundred of the tanks were now Panzer IIIs with the long-barrelled, high velocity 50mm gun, and 50 were the Panzer IVs with the even more powerful long 75mm gun.

The advantage of the desert was that it was mostly flat, with few towns or natural obstructions, but a stationary tank could be easily camouflaged. For tanks on the move, however, air cover was essential. Sand blown into the air by tank tracks could easily be detected by hostile aircraft and slow moving machines were an easy target from the air. The column of smoke from one burning tank identified the position of the unit from miles around.

For the tank crews the conditions in the desert which they had to endure were appalling. Insects were a perpetual torment. The heat inside the noisy, vibrating cabin was unbearable. The all-pervading sand caused engines to seize and turrets to jam. Sand penetrated the caterpillar tracks which then ground themselves apart. The heavy complicated machinery required continual maintenance and without their tank the crew were at the mercy of the unforgiving desert.

In battle the armour plating of the tanks protected the crew from rifle and machine gun fire and, to a varying extent, from shell fire. But even the best armoured tank was vulnerable to heavy and well-directed anti-tank fire. For many of the tank soldiers who perished in the sands,

German grenadiers inspect the knocked-out hulk of an American light tank in Tunisia in 1943.

death did not come easily. A tank sustaining a direct hit might simply explode, but if it didn't the energy of the impact was converted into intense heat resulting in a dramatic increase in temperature in the interior. Burns and asphyxiation claimed many lives. Rivets commonly used in the construction of heavy tanks were an additional hazard. A hit would cause rivets to burst out, pelting the crew with red hot metal. It was said that the screams of the dying trapped inside a blazing tank were never forgotten by those who heard them.

Even when men did manage to scramble out of a blazing tank in the desert they were frequently far from proper medical facilities and during engagements water for both fit and wounded was invariable in short supply.

Ahead lay the battle of El Alamein after which the Afrika Korps would be pursued to the final battles in Tunisia.

CAPTURED BRITISH TANKS

As the Afrika Korps began to retreat they also lost the battle for another important aspect of desert tank warfare: recovery and repair. Tanks knocked out in battles by shells, mines, or breakdown could not now be rescued on the retreat.

The allies always had numerical superiority in armoured fighting vehicles but axis forces managed to capture and utilise large numbers of allied equipment. For example, the axis victory at Benghazi in late January 1942 provided them with 96 tanks, 38 guns and some one hundred and ninety vehicles, of which a fair number were utilised. The German Afrika Korps was the most notable user of all kinds of captured equipment and it was reported that sometimes the inventory consisted of more captured equipment than that of German origin. On 12th February 1942 Panzer Abteilung z.b.V Panzer Armee Afrika, a special employment unit equipped entirely with captured British and American armoured fighting vehicles, was formed. The oldest British tank captured by the Germans in North Africa was Medium Tank Mk II, which entered service in 1925. The Medium Tank Mk II was an obsolete vehicle by any standards at the time and even the hard-pressed Germans couldn't bring themselves to use them in service.

The two man Light Tanks, Mk II A and Mk II B, were used during the early part of the North African Campaign and a small number were captured by the DAK and pressed into temporary service. The Mk II A and Mk II B received the German designation Leichter Panzerkampfwagen Mk II 733(e).

The two-man Light Tank Mk V was a further development of earlier light tanks, and also saw service in the early part of the North African Campaign. As with the Mk II A and Mk II B, the small number which were captured by the Afrika Korps were pressed into temporary service as Leichter Panzerkampfwagen Mk IV 734(e).

The DAK also utilised other British vehicles, which had been previously encountered in France. The Matilda II, designated as Infanterie Panzerkampfwagen Mk II 748(e), was one which saw extensive service on the German side in the desert war. In early August 1941 the 15th Panzer Division's 8th Panzer Regiment had one platoon entirely made up of captured tanks including seven Matilda IIs. One of the captured Matilda IIs was nicknamed 'Dreadnought' by its British crew. It was captured, along with six more, at Halfaya Pass in May 1941. In late August 1941 seven Matilda IIs were transferred from the 8th Paiver Regiment to the 33rd Panzer Pionere (engineer) Battalion and, as of November 1941, there were still five Matilda IIs in service. In June 1941 the 21st Panzer Division's Panzer Regiment also had one platoon equipped with captured tanks, including Matilda IIs, but in August 1941 only one was still in service. In July additional Matilda IIs were captured near Bardia. The best known photo of a captured Matilda II from the 21st Panzer Division's Panzer Regiment was taken when Allied soldiers (possibly New Zealanders) recaptured it. Matilda IIs were easily repaired by German workshops. Unserviceable vehicles were scrapped for spare parts, and in some cases spare parts were even shipped from France where large numbers of Matilda II tanks, captured in May 1940, were still available. Some Matilda IIs turrets were mounted in the Halfaya Pass on concrete emplacements as fortifications.

The Cruiser Tank Mk VI (AI 5) Crusader, was the development of an unsuccessful Mk V Covenanter. It inherited Mk V's poor armour protection and unreliability but still saw extensive service in North Africa from 1941. The Crusader was produced in five variants: Mk VI Crusader I armed with a two-pounder. Mk-VI Crusader 1 CS armed with a 3in Howitzer, Mk VI Crusader 11 armed with a two-pounder, Mk VI Crusader II CS armed with a three inch Howitzer, and the Mk VI Crusader III armed with a six-pounder. The first examples were captured as early as June 1941, and the Crusader received the German designation of Kreuzer Panzerkampfwagen Mk VI 746(e). A number of Crusaders were captured in good condition - due to the high incidence of mechanical breakdowns their crews often abandoned them. German repair shops were able to fix a number of them by using other Crusaders as sources for spare parts. In some cases parts were again shipped from France, where Crusader tanks captured in May 1940 were still available. Captured models of the Crusader type were pressed into either short-term service or long-term service, for example in the previously mentioned Panzer Abteilung z.b.V Panzer Armee.

The DAK had a platoon of Crusaders in service from February to December of 1942. Besides the vehicles in service with this unit, additional tanks were in service with a variety of units, including the 21st Panzer Division's 5th Panzer Regiment and the 90th Light African Division's 605th Panzerjäger Abteilung. A Number of Crusader tanks were captured after the Sollum battle of June 1941. When, on 13th May 1943 DAK surrendered, the few Crusaders which were still in service were recaptured. In general, the Germans liked Crusaders for their speed and manoeuvrability.

The British Infantry Tank Mk III Valentine was produced in eleven main variants designated Mk I to Mk XI. Allied forces in North Africa utilised the first five variants all armed with two-pounder (40mm) guns. The Valentine Mk I and Mk 11 were operated by a three-man crew, while the Mk III to Mk XI were operated by a four-man crew. The Germans designated Valentine as 'Infanterie Panzerkampfwagen Mk III 749(e)'. The Valentine was also used as a base for the Bishop self-propelled gun, armed with a 25-pounder (87.6mm) field gun, which also saw service in North Africa. In 1941/42 the Germans captured a number of Valentines, mainly Mk IIs. which were then pressed into service with (Beute) Panzer Abteilung z.b.V Panzer Armee Afrika, which had as many as 12 of them at any one time. Additionally, at least five Valentines were in service with the 90th Light African Division's 605th Panzerjäger Abteilung. A single Valentine was also shipped back to Kummersdorf for testing purposes. Probably the best known picture of a captured Valentine is that of a Mk V in service with 10th Panzer Division's 7th Panzer Regiment in Tunisia in early 1943. Unserviceable tanks were either scrapped for parts or were dug in as defensive positions. When the DAK surrendered, a few Valentines, which were still in service, were recaptured by their former owners.

Inside the tank works tracks are tested for use with the Panzer III.

The four-man American M3 Light Tank armed with 37mm gun was known to the British unofficially as the 'Honey' and to the Americans as the 'Stuart'. The Honey saw service with the British before the arrival of American troops in North Africa and then with Americans. Only a small number of Honey and Stuart light tanks were captured and pressed into service by DAK. They were designated as Panzerkampfwagen M3 740(a). On 22nd and 23rd November 1941 the 15th Panzer Division captured 35 Stuarts, most of which were badly damaged, near Gabr Saleh in Libya. A few were made serviceable and were maintained using spare parts from damaged vehicles. Twelve Stuart tanks captured in June 1942 were also pressed into service by the Panzer Company of Rommel's Kampfstaffel and remained in service as late as March 1943 in Tunisia. The M3 was followed by an improved version M5 Light Tank, also used in North Africa. Only a few M5 tanks were captured by DAK and temporarily used as Panzerkampfwagen M3 740(a).

The six-man American M3 Medium Tank was an interim solution before the introduction of M4 Sherman Medium Tank. It was produced in two versions designated as the 'Grant' and the 'Lee'. The Grant was a version produced with a British-designed turret and saw service with the British before the arrival of American troops in North Africa. The Lee was a standard version produced for the American Army. Both versions were armed with a turret-mounted 37mm gun and a hull-mounted 75mm gun. A Small number of M3 medium tanks were captured by DAK and pressed into temporary service as Panzerkampfwagen M3 747(a).

DIEPPE 1942

On 19 August 1942 allied forces made up mainly of Canadians performed an unsuccessful raid on the French port of Dieppe, code named Operation Jubilee. The raid was unsuccessful, with a high casualty rate because of the incorrect assessment of the German strength in the area including the presence of the 10th Panzer Division. The landing forces included some 30 Churchill tanks and some seven scout cars. Only 15 of the Churchills managed to leave the beaches before being stopped by roadblocks. It was, however, the first time that armoured fighting vehicles had taken part in an amphibious landing.

The five-man Infantry Tank Mk IV Churchill (A22) was largely based on experiences of the Western Front from 1914 to 1918, although the first was produced in May 1941. It was a slow and well-armoured tank with a design that resembled First World War tank mounted with a turret. The Churchill became the most important and successful of British tanks and was produced in ten main versions, along with a variety of special purpose tanks. Three main models of Churchills were used during the Dieppe raid. The Mk I was armed with a turret-mounted two-pounder (40mm) gun and a hull-mounted three inch (76.2mm) Howitzer. The Mk II had a machine gun instead of the Howitzer and the Mk III was armed with a turret-mounted six-pounder (57mm) gun. The Germans captured and salvaged 23 Churchill infantry tanks, most damaged after heavy fighting. The most numerous was Mk III, of which ten were acquired, along with five Mk II and six Mk I tanks, although only a few were in a state to be repaired. Vehicles beyond repair were scrapped for spare parts and then used for target practice or other training exercises. A single example of every model was transferred to the Army Weapons Office for evaluation and testing purposes. A small number of Churchills, mainly Mk III were taken into German service, including one Mk III nicknamed 'Blondie', previously commanded by Corporal Jordan. Churchills equipped the Captured Panzer Company, which in late 1942 became Panzer Regiment 100. In late 1943 there were still two Mk III tanks in service with Panzer Regiment 100 and they were eventually transferred to Panzer Abteilung 205 in early 1944. It was very hard to maintain Churchills in running condition since there were only spare parts available from scrapped tanks along with a limited supply of ammunition. One of the Mk III tanks was personally inspected by Albert Speer, the Minister for Armaments and Munitions. The Churchill received the German designation of Infanterie Panzerkampfwagen Mk IV(e).

BARBAROSSA

"Seven weeks of the most important and historic events are behind us. Stalin's main armies are shattered, his powerful Panzer forces are almost completely destroyed. The door to Moscow has been forced open, the Reds will not succeed in closing it again."

GENERALOBERST HOTHI, AUGUST 1941

The launch of Operation Barbarossa, the invasion of the Soviet Union, on 22nd June 1941, was Hitler's most desperate gamble of the Second World War. It was a gamble Hitler felt compelled to take, if his ambition of the complete subjugation of Europe was to become a reality. Four-fifths of Germany's total armies, three million men, were committed to the most appalling conflict in the history of warfare.

In 1941 the conquest of Russia would not only have provided Germany with the agricultural and industrial supplies to ensure Hitler's mastery of Europe, it would have simultaneously rid him of the only military power capable of challenging his domination. The deaths of tens of millions of Russians was not simple an economic necessity, their destruction would pave the way for the 'Grossraum', a concept already under development by Heinrich Himmler as the culmination of Hitler's call for 'Lebensraum'. The Grossraum was envisaged as a gigantic Germanic state stretching from the Atlantic Ocean in the west to the mountains of the Urals, in the east.

Standing between Hitler and the realisation of this vision were the armies of the Union of Soviet Socialist Republics, a fighting force whose condition of unpreparedness was a testament to the paranoia of its political leadership and the excesses of a state which vied with Germany in the

A propaganda image which has become on of the most famous of World War II is this study of a Panzer III from the 18th Panzer Division crossing the River Bug in June 1941.

extent of its totalitarian oppression. Hitler's first Barbarossa directive ominously stated that the USSR might be invaded even before the war with Great Britain was over.

Though Stalin accepted that war was now inevitable, he believed Russia had until the spring of 1942 to prepare herself. His fanatical rejection of counter-information was so fierce that vital intelligence concerning German preparations was kept from him by subordinates fearful of the violence of his reaction.

As the German build-up toward Operation Barbarossa continued. Stalin's attempts to pacify Hitler grew more desperate. He had already stated in an interview with PRAVDA in November 1939 that it was not Germany who had attacked Britain and France, but Britain and France who had attacked Germany. Stalin now forbade any criticism of Germany to be printed in the newspapers. He increased Russian supplies to Germany and withdrew recognition of the Norwegian and Belgian governments in exile. When Hitler successfully invaded Greece and Yugoslavia, Stalin expelled the Yugoslavian ambassador to Moscow and refused a request to recognise the Greek government in exile.

Stalin felt he was continuing to buy time by these unrequited concessions, but the breathing space he obtained was totally devoid of any worthwhile attempt to remedy his military disadvantages. By May 1940 170 Soviet divisions were stationed in newly occupied Polish territories, with the result that over half the army were occupying positions with fortifications and rearward communications which were incomplete. Indeed, by June, with a German attack imminent, Western Special Military District was a complete shambles.

Many formations were between six and seven thousand men short of wartime establishment. Numbers of experienced personnel had been hived off to build new tank and aviation units. Only one of six mechanised Corps had received their full complement of equipment. Three of the four motorised divisions had no tanks and four out of every five vehicles in the tank fleets were obsolete. Four of the Corps had only one quarter of their designated motor vehicles, and in another

Corps one in three motor vehicles needed repairs. Therefore, although the opposing forces had amassed vast amounts of weaponry along their common borders, the Soviet Red Army and the German Wehrmacht were anything but equal adversaries.

The awesome German armies, which the 170 under-strength divisions of the Russian troops faced, were divided into three large groups. These consisted of 148 fully manned and equipped divisions of which 19 were Panzer and 15 Panzer Grenadier divisions. The Army Group South was commanded by Field Marshall Gerd von Runstedt and was charged with seizing Kiev and taking control of the Ukraine as far as the river Dnieper. Field Marshall von Bock's Army Group Centre was to strike towards Smolensk. Army Group North under Field Marshall von Lieb was to attack through the Baltic States and seize Leningrad.

The three German army groups were supplemented by 500,000 Finnish troops advancing from their homeland in 14 divisions 150,000 Romanians attacking along the Black Sea towards Odessa. These forces, together with the Luftwaffe, which had devoted 80 per cent of its operational strength – 2,770 aircraft - to the build up of Barbarossa, fielded over three thousand three hundred and fifty tanks, over seven thousand artillery pieces, 60,000 motor vehicles and 625,000 horses.

There was, however, one vital flaw in the German organisation, previously mentioned - the questionable decision to reduce the tank strength of each of the divisions from a two-regiment brigade to a single regiment. At a stroke the tank strength of the division was reduced from 340 to 170 tanks. The initial compensation for the dilution of strength in the Panzer Divisions came in the form of the deployment of more Divisions. The resulting Panzer Divisions within each of the separate army groups were bought together to form miniature Panzer armies. By concentrating a number of Panzer divisions together the Germans were able to achieve a massive local superiority of numbers at the point of decision. In the early part of the campaign the far-sighted use of armoured formations went a great deal towards offsetting the dilution of the tank strengths of the Divisions.

The Russian army still clung to its peacetime structure. Should war occur, each military district would be transformed into army groupings similar in structure to the German forces opposing them. The Soviet Northern front was to repel advances through the Balkans and defend Leningrad from Finnish attack. The North-West, West and South-West fronts would engage the three main German army groups, and the Southern front would deal with any advance towards Odessa.

Behind these lines, the contrast between the warring nations could not have been greater. While Germany boasted one of the finest industrial infrastructures in the world, Russia had still not completed her industrial revolution. By 1941 a generation of upheaval had left its mark economically and psychologically. Revolution and civil war had been followed by the destruction of the peasantry and their enforced collectivisation. Whole segments of the population had been uprooted and transported to work the new industries set up in the mineral rich region of Siberia, the Urals and Kazakhstan.

At 4am on the 22nd June 1941 the maelstrom that was Barbarossa finally erupted. The German armies of the Blitzkrieg sliced through the Russian forces on every front. Faced by the results of his intransigent refusal to act, Stalin became frozen with indecision. While his army headquarters desperately tried to piece together the most rudimentary picture of what was happening, he ordered an immediate counter-offensive on all fronts. As the first reports of the devastation his own command had helped to create filtered through, he was shattered.

"All that Lenin created we have lost forever," he declared. He finally retreated to his dacha, not to emerge until 3rd July.

At the front, the concerted rapier thrusts of the German Panzer divisions were skewering through the chaotic Russian defences. The Panzer groups created deadly breaches in the Soviet line, slicing the Red Army forces into isolated segments. The supporting German divisions then moved forward in encircling advances which surrounded these pockets of defenders. The ferocity and effectiveness of the Panzer attacks were so great that some of the pockets were gigantic. Groups of up to fifteen Russian divisions were surrounded and mercilessly bludgeoned into surrender.

The encirclement of Minsk by the right flank of Army Group North and the left flank of Army Group Centre yielded 300,000 prisoners, 2,500 tanks and 1,400 artillery pieces. Thirty-two of the 43 Russian divisions were destroyed within a week and the road to Moscow penetrated to a depth of 300km.

The remainder of Army Group North led by Panzer Group IV, under Hoepner, scythed into the Baltic States, capturing Riga, the Latvian capital. Only in the south were the German forces

The effects of the long campaign have begun to show on these Panzer IIIs halted in a Russian village just before the onset of winter 1941.

limited to shallow advances toward Lvov and Rovno.

On the ground chaos reigned. The Luftwaffe were pulverising the road and rail links behind the Russian lines. Many Russian officers were not even using code in their desperate radio requests for instructions from their headquarters. Struggling masses of uncoordinated troops were being slaughtered by the German troops as they attempted to obey Stalin's orders to counter-attack. Others were being machine-gunned by their own military police for fleeing from positions which were worse than hopeless.

By 3rd July the battle for the frontier was over. The German armies had advanced along a line from the river Dvina in the north to the Dnieper in the south. General Halder, Chief of German General Staff, declared that the war against the Soviet Union had taken only 14 days to win. But German intelligence had totally underestimated the reserves which Russia could command. By 1st July 5,300,000 men had been mobilised and Stalin had emerged from his isolation to broadcast a message of patriotism and resistance to the nation. For once, the Russian people were told the truth. The pre-war complacency which Stalin had done so much to foster had rapidly to be undone. Stalin now took direct control of the Red Army. But the general mobilisation of Russian troops failed to curtail the German advance.

Four reserve armies of 37 divisions were despatched to holster West Front in the general area of Smolensk. The Germans countered with yet another encirclement and the Panzer groups of Generals Hoth and Guderian smashed through the Soviet line and manoeuvred 300,000 Russian troops into an indefensible pocket. Another 150,000 prisoners, 2,000 tanks and 2,000 artillery pieces fell into German hands.

Goebbels announced that: "The eastern continent lies like a limp virgin in the mighty arms of the German Mars".

Army Group South finally broke through the Russian South-West Front and another pocket yielded a further toll of 100,000 prisoners.

WITTMANN JOINS THE FRAY

Although the war in Russia began with Operation Barbarossa towards the end of June, the Leibstandarte wasn't initially committed, so the war in the Soviet Union for Michael Wittmann actually began a month later, in July 1941. It was like a second baptism of fire for Wittmann, who faced an attack by 18 Russian tanks on his Sturmgeschütz Battery's first day in action.

He had encountered nothing like this in Poland and Greece, but Wittman was a natural fighter and he succeeded in knocking out six enemy tanks in succession. The rest fled the field in disarray. This was Wittmann's first striking success, and the incident provided the first signs of his supreme talent as commander of an armoured fighting vehicle.

On 12 July 1941, in recognition of his great feat on his first day in action in Russia, Wittmann was decorated with the Iron cross - Second Class.

But there was little time for celebration, as the advance continued.

The short 75mm gun of the German Assault gun in the early war years was an inferior weapon to the long 76mm gun of the Russian T-34 tanks, but despite this disadvantage Wittmann proved himself a master of armoured warfare.

Combat in Russia placed terrific demands on the assault gun crews. Frequently, Wittmann and his crew were on their own, separated from the rest of the assault gun battery. In this hostile environment, he showed himself to be a successful lone fighter with initiative. Nevertheless, he remained popular with his comrades. Wittmann's gunner at that time, Otto Schalte, described him as a modest man;

"Michael was a quiet, gifted, friendly NCO with firm goals in front of him."

With 2,000 miles of front to fight over, the German armoured forces were spread incredibly thinly. It was lucky for Wittmann that he was such a good lone warrior, as the assault guns were rarely employed en masse, as the standing orders required, so his skills were forged in the hard battles of the summer of 1941. Unit commanders were always happy to have an assault gun

The men of the Panzertruppen were as ill-prepared as the rest of the German army for the onset of the Russian winter. These men are wearing 1941 pattern greatcoats which proved to be hopelessly inadequate for the conditions. In the case of the vehicles the situation was even worse; neither lubricants nor machinery had been designed to withstand the conditions they were about to face.

assigned to their sector, particularly one commanded by him.

The German advance along the Black Sea began in the first weeks of August 1941. Wittmann fought near Sasselje and Nowyj Bug from the 10th-17th August and on the 19th at Kherson. In the course of the fighting for the port city of Kherson, a bizarre incident took place as the assault guns commanded by Wittmann and Beck engaged first an enemy gunboat, then a submarine. The gunboat was sunk, but the effects of the fire directed at the submarine are not recorded.

Wittmann had destroyed ten enemy tanks by this point in his career. But his luck was about to change for the worse, as a direct hit on his vehicle, though it failed to penetrate the armour, nonetheless left Wittmann wounded in the face and back by shell fragments. However, Wittman's tally continued to rise to 25 enemy tanks and 32 anti-tank guns destroyed. Yet combat losses were not just on the Russian side. Those on his own also rose steadily.

In February 1942 the depleted assault gun battery was brought up to battalion strength through new additions from Germany, and the transfer of a battery from the SS Wiking Division.

As a result of this expansion, Wittmann was made an SS officer candidate in early 1942. He left the battalion in June in order to attend the Candidate Training Course at the SS-Junkerschule in Bad Tolz. Wittmann learned tactical lessons which he combined with his practical battlefield experience. The 28-year old Wittman now served as Platoon Commander in the 2nd Company of the SS Panzer Replacement Battalion.

TOWN AND STREET FIGHTING

For the tank men the opening weeks of the offensive had gone like clockwork. However, all of the lessons From the Polish campaign had obviously not been fully assimilated and the German forces once again found themselves drawn into fighting for towns and cities, with resulting high casualties in men and machines.

In attacking a town or village, the German tactics were to employ flanking and encircling tactics. They attempted to cut off water, electricity, gas, and other utilities. While carrying out the flanking manoeuvre, they tried to pin down the defenders with heavy artillery fire and aerial bombardment. When it was necessary to make a direct assault, the German tactics were to concentrate all available heavy weapons, including artillery and air units, on one target. They favoured as targets for their massed fire the forward edges of the community, especially detached groups of buildings and isolated houses. During the artillery fire concentration the infantry would assemble and attack their objective immediately upon termination of artillery barrage. Tanks and assault guns accompanied the infantry, and with their fire immobilised any new enemy forces which appeared. They also supported the infantry in sweeping away barricades, blasting passages through walls and crushing wire obstacles. Guns and mortars were used against concealed positions, with anti-tank guns to cover side streets against possible flanking operations. Machine guns engaged snipers on roofs.

The immediate objective of the German thrust into a built-up area was to divide the area occupied by the enemy. These areas were then isolated into as many smaller areas as possible, in order to deny freedom of movement.

Russian armoured warfare was inhibited by Stalin's disenchantment with tank divisions, which had led him in the 30's to utilise his armour only in the support of infantry formations. After witnessing German successes on the western front, Stalin changed his mind, but a reorganisation on that scale meant that the reshuffle of Russian armour was not completed before the launch of Barbarossa. Even though Russian tanks outnumbered German two to one at the front and six to one overall, tactical ineffectiveness, obsolete models and widespread disrepair tipped the advantage overwhelmingly in favour of Germany during the first stages of the conflict.

But ground forces were only part of a Blitzkrieg operation, which saw German advances of up to fifty miles per day. The fast-moving Panzer Groups were again supported by Junkers Ju-87 two-seater bombers, which were protected by Messerschmit 109 fighters. The Ju-87, more familiarly known as the Stuka, was one of the most versatile machines of all time. Used as a night bomber, torpedo launcher, trainer, long range reconnaissance aircraft and for a host of other specialist taasks, it was at its most fearsome as a dive-bomber. Screeching out of the sky like some furious bird of prey, its air brakes allowed it to slow to a speed which enabled its bomb load to be delivered with almost pinpoint accuracy.

THE ADVANCE CONTINUES

After a month of victorious progress, the German High Command were disconcerted by the rapidity of their own advance. Their armies were now fighting on a front 1,000 miles wide. The Stukas could no longer deliver the concerted hammer blows which had punched the holes in the Russian lines which the Panzers had so mercilessly exploited. Even though the Soviet airforce had by now lost approximately five thousand aircraft, the supply of replacements seemed endless. The factories in the east, which were churning out more effective fighter models, were out of Luftwaffe bombing range. The German air assault began to run low on fighters.

The Luftwaffe also had serious supply problems. The distance from home base and the destruction of the transport infrastructure meant that aircraft replacement pans had to be flown to forward airfield. The lengthening supply lines were also affecting the German ground forces. Tank commanders, hundreds of miles from their Polish depots, nevertheless pressed for the final thrust toward Moscow. They argued that only the continuation of the offensive would prevent the Russians from organising a fresh line of resistance. While many of Hitler's generals disagreed that such an attack should be launched immediately, they were almost unanimous in recommending that Moscow should become the primary objective of the next phase of the war.

Hitler, on the other hand, was worried about the possibility of the gaps between the Panzer divisions and the main armies being exploited by Russian reinforcements. He also feared that the hundreds of thousands of Soviet troops left behind the German lines in the wake of the advance might co-ordinate their actions into an effective guerrilla movement.

Hitler had never been fully convinced of the importance of Moscow and continued to regard it as a secondary objective. The debate stretched out until mid-August. A vital month of summer weather was wasted. The Russians had the breathing space to throw reserve divisions into the gaps in their defences. Though barely trained, poorly equipped, some in the battered remnants of their civilian clothing, their stubborn ferocity meant that they were still a force to be reckoned with.

Eventually, the generals were silenced and two major objectives were prioritised: the capture of Moscow and the fall of the Ukraine.

A giant pincer movement, involving Guderian's Panzer Group II in a movement from the North and Panzer Group I under von Kleist who were to sweep up from the south, began to close its jaws on a huge pocket of Russian forces to the rear of Kiev. Field Marshall Zhukov, the Soviet Chief of Staff, pleaded with Stalin for a strategic withdrawal of the troops defending the city. He was dismissed from his post. Marshall Timoshenko, the newly appointed South-West commander, arrived just in time to see the Soviet divisions trapped. The 600,000 prisoners taken by the Germans remain the highest number ever captured in a single engagement.

The battle for the Ukraine now centred on the Crimean Peninsula where the right flank of Army Group South pressed the Soviet 51st army back towards Sebastapol. While half of the German Group Centre were engaged in subduing the Ukraine, Marshall Zhukov was transferred to the reserve forces behind West Front, and seized the opportunity to attack the German 4th army. Occupying a salient near Smolensk, the Germans were now themselves vulnerable to encirclement. The 4th army were thrown back 12km but, without sufficient tanks and aircraft, Zhukov failed to tighten the noose he had made. However, in terms of morale, Zhukov's counter thrust was highly significant. His action was the first substantial Soviet counter-attack of the war.

Hitler's response was to regroup Army Group Centre and prepare the most critical operation of the campaign. Operation Typhoon, the drive toward Moscow, was finally under way. Seventy divisions, spearheaded by the 1,500 tanks of Panzer Groups 2 and 3, would race toward the Russian capital before the rains of autumn or the snows of winter could halt their progress.

On 30th September General Heinz Guderian's 2nd Panzer Group almost inevitably broke through the Soviet line and had encircled the defending Bryansk Front by 6th October. Simultaneously, the Western Front, commanded by Marshall Timoshenko, fell into a similar trap. The pockets of Vyazma and Bryansk containing nine armies of 71 divisions were almost completely destroyed. Another 660,000 troops faced the grim brutality that the German army meted out to prisoners of war and the road to Moscow lay open.

In the Baltic States von Lieb's Army Group North had captured the city of Novgorod by 16th August, a vital target in the approach to Leningrad. The beleaguered defenders had fought to the death following the German discovery of the city's defensive plans on the corpse of a Soviet officer. General Hoepner's 4th Panzer Group resumed its drive toward Leningrad, but without supporting infantry its progress was limited.

Men of the 11th Panzer Division advance cautiously through the streets of a Russian village in December 1941.

Leningrad was a vital centre of the wartime production industry, and reserves and equipment were poured into the defence of the city. The citizens themselves formed into militia, divisions of which were flung against the Germans more in despair than hope. Following a basic training period averaging 16 hours, the first militia divisions were sent to the front, six days after being formed; the second two days, and the third, the same day it was established.

Despite such gargantuan efforts, the first shells began to pour down on Leningrad early in September. With the arrival of the 18th Army to reinforce the Panzers on the 8th, the German stranglehold on the city tightened further. The capture of Schlusselburg to the east signalled the end of rail transport.

When Marshall Zhukov arrived to take

A mixed force of Panzer IIs and IIIs halt for the night in a Russian village at the time of Operation Typhoon in December 1941.

over the defence of the city on 10th September, he found the defenders in an advanced state of disorganisation and the inhabitants close to panic. Undaunted, he briskly set about bolstering its defences. A shortage of anti-tank guns was dealt with by converting anti-aircraft artillery to the task of attempting to halt the Panzers. Six brigades of naval infantry and students were formed and reinforcements drafted in from the Karelian Isthmus. Zhukov began to take the fight to the Germans, through raids and counter-attacks, but by now the German troops had pierced the inner circle of defences and were rampaging through the suburbs.

After a furious exchange of advances and retreats, at the end of the month the defenders were still hanging on to their city by their fingernails. It seemed inevitable that Leningrad would capitulate.

But as Zhukov awaited a renewed assault, the 4th Panzer Group suddenly departed. They had been ordered south to join the battle for Moscow and the remaining German forces began to build siege lines. Leningrad would not now be taken by force, it would be starved into submission.

The German invaders now controlled all of western Russia on a line from Leningrad in the north to Rostov on the Black Sea, and the Red Army was still retreating before them. The countryside they left behind was a wasteland. The first few months of the war had robbed the nation of nearly fifty per cent of her grain-producing lands.

But the fighting spirit of the Russians was far from crushed. It had been inflamed by accounts of the slaughter of prisoners of war, and the murder and torture committed by the German invaders. Even the constant series of military reverses failed to dampen the ardour of defenders whose motherland had been ravaged.

THE T-34 MENACE

When Hitler ordered the conquest of Russia in the summer of 1941, confidence among the Panzer force was at an all time high. The desert war was progressing well and the German tactics of mixing tank and anti-tank forces together concealed the deficiencies in tank design, in some cases from the Germans themselves.

Despite the understandable cockiness of the German High Command, a few lessons from earlier campaigns had been absorbed, and the make-up of the tank force which shook Stalin to the core had a much higher proportion of the heavier Mark III and IV tanks, instead of the lightweight

A Panzer IV being guided into a concealed position in a Russian forest.

Panzer Is and IIs. This trend illustrated the steadily increasing reliance on heavier armour, which was to continue throughout the war. It was just as well, because the Wehrmacht was about to meet with a very nasty surprise.

After a few weeks of the campaign, during which the German armour had faced only obsolete Russian tanks such as the lumbering T-28 and the outdated BT-7, the German forces suddenly encountered two of the new Russian tanks which were to change the course of the war.

The first was the Heavy KV-1, a 46-ton monster, with superior heavy armour and a vicious 76mm gun capable of destroying any German tank from most ranges on the battlefield. In 1941 this was a deadly adversary indeed.

The Soviet KV-1 was a fine example of a tank made for specific conditions. It had broad tracks for dealing with mud and snow, and a diesel engine for operating in the coldest possible weather. It was a superb design and absolutely dominated the battlefield.

The other unpleasant surprise for the Germans was, of course, the arrival of the T-34, a medium tank far better armed and equipped than the German Mark IV. It was also better equipped to deal with the extreme Russian weather conditions. Its wide tracks made it equally at home in dry conditions or in the mud and snow. In addition, the sloping armour presented an angled front to German fire, designed to cause shells to glance off the armour.

The T-34 was to become the real nemesis of the German army. It was built for mass assembly, and the crude welding lines can be clearly seen on surviving examples. It was no beauty but it was tough, and it possessed a rare in-built ability to be upgraded as the situation changed.

When the T-34 first appeared in service it was fitted with a 76mm gun and had a two-man crew in the turret. By 1944, the Soviets had not only up-gunned the tank to an 88mm weapon, they had also increased the turret size to enable it to take three men, which made for a far more efficient tank on the battlefield.

Although the Germans would devise better tanks, they could never hope to compete in terms of the sheer number of T-34s.

The T-34 was the most prolific tank of the Second World and when we consider that the Soviets achieved that and moved their tank producing facilities right across the country under German pressure, it really is a remarkable achievement. The workmanship was crude enough to make the average British or American factory worker weep, but that was not the main concern for the Russians. They were out to produce as many reliable, tough fighting tanks as possible, and in the T-34 they achieved it.

Time and time again veterans of the Russian front will praise the T-34. Sixty years later, Russian Front veteran Gerhard Majewski recalled the effectiveness of the machines he fought against.

"The T-34 at its time was by far and away the best tank the world had ever seen. It was actually second to none. The shape is followed even to this day - the outline of the tank. It was the mother so to speak of all modern tanks. It was just right in every respect, the guns, the armour, the speed, the lot."

The T-34 was by no means the best tank to emerge from the Second World War, but it was more than adequate for the task and the huge numbers manufactured would ultimately tip the balance of the whole war.

THE KV-1 IN ACTION

It was now, almost too late, that the German High Command began to urgently request new tanks with superior armour and more effective guns, to combat the KV-1 and T-34. This report, from a unit of Panzer Group IV facing the KV-1 for the first time, gives a clear indication of just how unprepared the German forces were when faced with the new breed of Russian armour:

"The Russian armoured force played only a subordinate role at the beginning of the war. In the advance of 1941, our troops encountered only small units which supported the infantry in the same manner as our own self-propelled assault guns. The Russian tanks operated in a very clumsy manner and were quickly eliminated by our anti-tank weapons. The Russians carried out counter¬attacks with large tank forces, either alone or in combined operations with other arms, only at individual, important sectors.

On 23rd June 1942 our 4th Panzer Group, after a thrust from East Prussia, had readied the Dubysa and had formed several bridgeheads. The defeated enemy infantry units scattered into the extensive forests and high grain fields, where they constituted a threat to our supply lines. As early as 25th June the Russians launched a surprise counter-attack on the southern bridgehead in the direction of Raseiniai with their hastily brought-up XIV Tank Corps. They overpowered the 6th Motorcycle Battalion which was committed in the bridgehead, took the bridge, and pushed on in the direction of the city. Our 114th Armoured Infantry Regiment, reinforced by two artillery battalions and 100 tanks, was immediately put into action and stopped the main body of enemy forces. Then there suddenly appeared, for the first time, a battalion of heavy enemy tanks of a previously unknown type. The tanks overran the armoured infantry regiment and broke through into the artillery position. The projectiles of all defence weapons (except the 88mm flak) bounced off the thick enemy armour.

The one hundred German tanks were unable to check the 20 Russian Dreadnoughts, and suffered losses. Several Czech-built tanks of the type 35(t) which had bogged down in the grain fields because of mechanical trouble, were flattened by the enemy monsters. The same fate befell a 150mm medium howitzer battery which kept on firing until the last minute. Despite the fact that it scored numerous direct hits from as close a range as 200 yards, its heavy shells were unable to put even a single tank out of action. The situation became critical. Only the 88mm flak finally knocked out a few of the Russian KV-1s and force the others to withdraw into the woods.

One of the KV-1s even managed to reach the only supply route of our task force located in the northern bridgehead, and blocked it for several days. The first unsuspecting trucks to arrive with supplies were immediately shot afire by the tank.

There were practically no means of eliminating the monster. It was impossible to bypass it because of the swampy surrounding terrain. Neither supplies nor ammunition could be brought up. The severely wounded could not be removed to the hospital for the necessary operations, so they died. The attempt to put the tank out of action with the 50mm anti-tank gun battery, which had just been introduced at that time, at a range of 500 yards, ended with heavy losses to crews and equipment of the battery. The tank remained undamaged in spite of the fact that, as was later determined, it got fourteen direct hits. These merely produced blue spots on its armour. When a camouflaged 88mm flak gun was brought up, the tank calmly permitted it to be put into position at a distance of 700 yards, and then smashed it and its crew before it was even ready to fire. The attempt of engineers to blow it up at night likewise proved abortive.

An early version of the Stug III moving up in support of the infantry through a blazing Soviet landscape.

To be sure, the engineers managed to get to the tank after midnight, and laid the prescribed demolition charge under the caterpillar tracks. The charge went off according to plan, but was insufficient for the oversized tracks. Pieces were broken off the tracks, but the tank remained mobile and continued to molest the rear of the front and to block all supplies. At first it received supplies at night from scattered Russian groups and civilians, but we later prevented this procedure by blocking off the surrounding area. However, even this isolation did not induce it to give up its favourable position. It finally became the victim of a ruse. Fifty tanks were ordered to feign an attack from three sides and to fire on it so as to draw all of its attention in those directions. Under the protection of this feint it was possible to set up and camouflage another 88mm flak gun to the rear of the tank, so that this time it actually was able to fire. Of the 12 direct hits scored by this medium gun, three pierced the tank and destroyed it."

To combat the KV-1 and the T-34 a new heavy tank was needed urgently, but, in the form of the Tiger, it wouldn't be available for at least a year.

To further compound matters, mistaken assessments based on experience in France, had led to even the heaviest German tank, the Mark IV, still being equipped with the short barrelled 75mm guns which were developed for the infantry support role. While Germany scrambled to produce the new heavy tanks, the Mk IVs were urgently re-equipped with long barrelled 75mm guns which gave them the high velocity which was required to deal with the T-34. Extra welded steel skirts were also added as defence against the new Russian hollow charged weapons.

Measures like these helped to keep up the momentum of the German advance in 1942 but, all the while, the Panzer Divisions were increasingly hard pressed by the growing numbers of T-34s and KV1s. Guderian himself, in November 1941, ran into a T-34 ambush and he witnessed his force being completely destroyed. It was then that the Germans began to realise they were up against something which they had not counted on.

In the German Reich it was felt that the deadly 88mm anti-tank gun was the ideal weapon for the task of destroying the hordes of T-34s. But the '88' was originally designed as an anti-aircraft gun. It was very large and not designed to be carried in the turret of a tank. What the Germans now needed was a tank big enough to house such a gun and well armoured enough to withstand the punishment which it would receive on the battlefield. It would take time to develop such a

Photographic proof that even the legendary T-34 was not equal to the Russian terrain. These three machines were bogged-down in marshy ground and abandoned by their crews. The wooden planks used to try and free the top machine are still visible.

machine and, in 1941, one stop-gap measure was to increase the production of assault guns in the form of the Sturmgeschütze, which utilised the Panzer in chassis and now also carried a high velocity 75mm gun.

There were two big advantages to the Sturmgeschütze. Firstly they were quicker and cheaper to produce, and secondly, they could actually fit a far larger gun than could normally be fitted into the turret of the Panzer III. The disadvantage, of course, was that the

Sturmgeschütze would never be as effective in open battle as the Russian tanks. It had no turret to swing round, and to fire in a different direction meant moving the whole vehicle round.

In 1941 the puny 50mm gun was still the standard anti-tank armament for German Panzer III tanks. The experience of tank ace Herman Bix was typical of the desperate straits many German tank commanders now found themselves in. Bix saw a dozen of his shells bounce off a KV-1 even at the closest ranges. Eventually he managed to silence the steel monster as it swung its turret to take aim against him by the expedient of a well aimed shot deliberately fired through the barrel of his opponents main gun.

Men like Bix were part of a new breed of German tank commanders who achieved incredible victories against superior forces. But these superior forces were now also armed with better equipment and a deadly race would now develop between the Russian capacity to manufacture more tanks and the Germans' ability to engineer better tanks. Although the German engineers would prove themselves winners, they were let down by their manufacturing capacity. The German war effort was being run inefficiently and by 1942 Germany was being targeted by wave after wave of allied bombers which were reducing her war industries to rubble, while Stalin had wisely moved his factories back into the interior of Russia, out of harm's way. The workers from one tank factory actually walked along railway lines under German gunfire to get in the trains to be moved out. It was the largest industrial migration in the history of the world; well over one thousand nine hundred plants were moved eastwards.

GERMAN COMMAND TANKS

To compensate for the low quality of their guns, the Germans further extended then technological lead by refining the special command tanks which had the main guns removed to make room for additional radio equipment.

These command tanks (Befehlspanzer) were factory conversions of ordinary gun tanks which were used by relatively senior tank commanders at squadron, company, battalion or regiment level to observe and to coordinate the actions of their subordinates on the battlefield. Command tanks generally mounted extra wireless sets, for these purposes, and in order to incorporate these extra wireless sets and sometimes extra wireless operators, something usually had to be removed from the tank. Generally speaking this was either ammunition, which is extremely bulky, or the main armament of the tank itself. Obviously removing either, and particularly the main gun, considerably disadvantaged a command tank on the battlefield.

The cohesion which came from the smooth flow of commands was one of the obvious reasons that the inferior German tanks of 1941 and 1942 were able to overcome the superior T-34s and KV-1s, but these command tanks soon drew special attention and attempts were made to disguise them with dummy guns - a length of wood or pipe, fashioned to represent the main gun.

Even when a dummy gun was used, however, the extra wireless antennae needed were another way with which the enemy could identify enemy command tanks and knock them out. This disconcerting factor was not mitigated by the rigid German practice of numbering their tanks in sequence, starting with the commander's vehicle, which frequently carried the number 001, displayed prominently on the turret - a sure invitation!

During 1942, the Red Army's armada of T-34s was growing ominously. New Russian tank armies were coming into being, and in the wake of the terrible defeat at Stalingrad the German soldiers prayed for an answer. It was now a race between German engineering and Soviet manufacturing.

CAPTURED RUSSIAN TANKS

As the war progressed, a large number of captured Soviet T-60s were pressed into service by the Germans but rarely as combat tanks. The majority were used as light and medium artillery tractors with or without turrets designated as Gepanzerter Artillerie Schlepper T-60(r).

The T-70 light tank was designed as a replacement for the T-60; although it was an improved version, it was also operated by just a two-man crew, but its armament consisted of a turret-mounted 45mm gun and a 7.62mm machine gun. According to original German captured tank inventories, as of July 1943 there was only one T-70(r) as part of Army Group South and three tanks as part of Army Group Centre.

The Germans found the BT series tanks to be technically unreliable, but they were able to maintain a number of them by using other tanks for spare parts. Some BT series tanks were still in service in 1944. As of 15th October 1941, there were officially ten BT series tanks in service with German units: the 1st Panzer Division had two BTs, the 8th Panzer Division had three BT-7s and the 19th Panzer Division had five BTs. A number of BT tanks were also known to be in service with the 3rd SS (Motorised) Division, 'Totenkopf' and 4th SS Polizei Panzer Grenadier Division. BT series tanks were used a combat tanks until 1942, when they were relegated to second line duties, including policing and security, in the Ukraine and Byelorussia. They were still in service in 1944.

The T-28 Medium Tank was a six-man lightly armoured tank inspired by the British Vickers-Armstrong A6 Medium Tank. It was produced in four versions. There is no evidence of them being used by the Germans, but possibly a number were used as fixed fortifications, while the rest were scrapped.

Along with other tanks, the Soviet Army had two main heavy tanks in service as at 22nd June 1941. These included some forty T-35 and approximately five hundred of the KV series heavy tanks.

The T-35 Heavy Tank was a 10-11 man multi-turreted tank inspired, to some extent, by the British Vickers A1E1 Independent Tank. It was produced in two versions and was armed with a single 76.2mm L/24 gun, two 37mm (model 1933) or two 45mm (model 1937) guns and six 7.62mm DT machine guns installed in five turrets. A number of these lumbering machines were captured intact by the Germans, either abandoned by their crews, or broken down through lack of fuel. The T-35A (model 1933) was an early production model designated by the Germans as Panzerkampfwagen T-35A 751°, while T-35C (model 1937) was a late production model with conical turrets and was designated by the Germans as Panzerkampfwagen T-35C 752(r). It is also possible that in the confusion designation of Panzerkampfwagen T-35C 752(r) was also given to the SMK heavy tank (named after Sergius Mironovitch Kirov), which was a prototype of a T-35 replacement, eventually abandoned. T-35 tanks were of great of interest to the Germans, who inspected them carefully and took numerous pictures, although there is no evidence of them being used in combat. Possibly a few were used as fixed fortifications, while the majority were scrapped. It is also reported that the few that were kept in reserve were used by the Germans in the defence of Konigsberg, Berlin and Kummersdorf in 1945.

In addition to the KV-1 there were also KV-2 close support tanks armed with turret-mounted 152mm howitzer. The main armament was installed in a large slab-sided high turret and the vehicle was operated by a six-man crew. Two versions were produced: KV-2A model in 1940 and improved KV-2B model in 1941. The Germans designated captured KV-2 tanks as Sturmpanzer KV-2 754(r). Only a few were pressed into service because of their limited combat value and the need for constant maintenance. The most publicised captured KV-2 tank was taken near Dubno by the 2nd Battalion of the Regiment 'General Goring' on 29th June 1941. It was painted with this message '2 ./Regiment General-Goring donated to our Führer! Dubno 24.6.41'. This machine became the subject of numerous propaganda photographs and newsreels. In addition to the Dubno machine it is also known that 8th Panzer division used a single KV-2 in the winter of 1942. Along with a single KV-1, another KV-2 was also shown during special exhibitions in

Germany. This particular KV-2 was found in the Krupp factory in Essen in 1945, where it was used for target practice. A number of KV-2 tanks were extensively tested at Kummersdorf, while seven were ordered to be maintained in perfect condition for unknown reasons. Badly damaged tanks were used for spare parts and eventually scrapped. In 1942 a single KV-2 and a T-34/76 were used to form 66th Panzer Company for the planned Invasion of Malta, code-named Herkules. Overall, the Germans only pressed the KV-2 into limited and temporary service. According to original German captured tank inventories of July 1943, there was only one KV-2(r) as part of Army Group Centre.

THE STURMGESCHÜTZ IN RUSSIA

The Sturmgeschütz made a valuable contribution to the success of Operation Barbarossa, but, despite the initial successes, by late 1941 it was apparent that the German armoured force as a whole was seriously under-gunned. The armoured forces of the Wehrmacht were in danger of being swamped by the new Russian T-34 tanks.

We have seen that the short 75mm gun of the Sturmgeschütz was really designed to fire low velocity, high explosive shells in support of infantry formations, and although it used the relatively small chassis of the Panzer III, the fact that it had no turret allowed the Stug to be up-gunned to incorporate the deadly long-barrelled 75mm gun, which could not be fitted to a Panzer III.

With this gun, the Sturmgeschütz was now a match for the T-34, and much more than an infantry support weapon. It was now apparent that, with its low silhouette, the Stug was a much harder target to hit than the Russian T-34. The sloped armour also helped to deflect shots away from the vehicle, and the scales gradually began to tip back in Germany's favour during the fierce tank battles of 1942.

This much-needed upgrade was first incorporated into the Sturmgeschütz Model F in 1942. The long barrelled L/43 gun gave the armour piercing shells fired by the Geschutz a much higher muzzle velocity and therefore a far greater tank killing capability than the 50mm gun of the Panzer III. It was now obvious that the Panzer III had evolved as far as it could and the model

This artist's impression conveys something of the shock which the German tank forces experienced under attack by the KV-1 for the first time. The superior power and armour of the KV-1 is well represented in this dramatic but accurate propaganda drawing for Signal magazine.

was phased out. From 1943 the Panzer III chassis was used exclusively for the manufacture of Sturmgeschütze, production of which continued right up to the last days of the war.

The pressure of battle on the Eastern Front ensured that, almost by accident, the German forces had evolved a very successful example of a new breed of fighting vehicle - the Panzerjäger or Tank Hunters. It was in this role that most Sturmgeschütze were to be employed for the rest of the war, and 20,000 enemy tank kills were claimed by assault gun crews up to the early months of 1944.

The Sturmceschutze manual stressed time and time again the need for the gun to be stationary when firing. In this way the highest level of accuracy was achieved. When the commanders heeded this request, the results were devastating.

In a mobile battle, where every second counts, the lack of a turret was a very real disadvantage, but Sturmgeschütze crews learned to adopt defensive tactics designed to lure Russian tanks into carefully constructed killing grounds.

The new tactics certainly worked, and in early 1943 there was another increase in gun power with introduction of the long 48 calibre gun, which gave extra velocity.

It was this new gun which equipped the definitive Sturmgeschütze, the Model G, of which 7720 were eventually manufactured. The sheer number produced is a reflection of just how effective and popular it was in battle.

By comparison to the 11,500 Sturmgeschütze manufactured, only 4,500 Panzer Ills, 6,800 Panzer Ivs and 6,000 Panthers were manufactured in the same period.

While the turreted tanks took on the role of the battlefield rovers, designed to forge ahead of the infantry in wide ranging strategic advances, it was the Sturmgeschütze which accompanied the Grenadiers during the dogged fighting on the ground. As the war dragged on, they became the infantry's rock in defence and his armoured fist in attack.

By 1943 the Sturmgeschütz was an indispensable part of both the Panzer Division and the ordinary infantry division. The infantry soon came to know that as long as the Gerschutze were in line, things were in control.

Extraordinary results were achieved by skilled crews in Russia, who sometimes accounted for dozens of Russian machines in a single action. In those actions, a major issue for the Sturmgeschütze commanders was the limited fuel and ammunition capacity of their cramped vehicles which produced a constant need to leave the battlefield. As the war progressed, the soldiers in the front line increasingly took strength from the presence of the Geschutze, so the tactical manual for their employment went to great lengths to stress the importance of the Sturmgeschütz commander keeping his infantry commanders informed that his guns were leaving the line only to re-arm and re-fuel.

It was a standard rule of Sturmgeschütz tactical doctrine that, if possible, not all machines would be withdrawn from the line at the same time, but that they should leave the field in relays, otherwise there was a real danger that the morale of the infantry might collapse if they saw their beloved Geschutze withdrawing from the field.

Despite its undoubted success as a tank killer, there was still an infantry support role for the Sturmgeschütz. The low trajectory 75mm gun was an excellent anti-tank gun, but to reach infantry hiding behind obstacles or other terrain features, a high trajectory Howitzer was still required. A further 1,100 Sturmgeschütze were therefore manufactured with the 10.5cm Howitzer which packed a deadly, high explosive punch which could be used in support of the infantry, either in attack or (more usually) desperate defence. The theory was that for every two troops of 75mm armoured Geschutze to deal with enemy tanks, there would be one troop of howitzer-armoured Geschutze to deal with the infantry. Problems with supplies of vehicles meant that this situation was very rarely achieved in practice.

The tactics set down for cooperation between the two types of assault guns was that the guns armed with 7.5cm guns would target any enemy armour, while the howitzer-armoured vehicles would concentrate on the infantry who accompanied the tanks. In this way, countless Russian attacks came to on the bulwark provided by the Sturmgeschütze battalions.

By 1943 the obvious success of the Sturmgeschütz in the field led the allies to target the

Alkett factory responsible tor the production of Stug IIIs for priority bombing. The resultant saturation bombing severely damaged the production factories.

During the period of rebuilding production was switched from Alkett to the Krupp's tank works, but Krupp made Panzer IVs not Panzer IIIs.

During 1943 the 1500 Sturmgeschütze manufactured by Krupp used the Panzer IV tank chassis, combined with the highly successful L/48 gun. These machines, known as Sturmgeschütze IVs, were no less successful than the old Stug IIIs.

By the end of the war over thirty thousand enemy tanks had been destroyed by the Geschutze crews, a ratio of approximately three enemy vehicles to every Stug deployed. It was a mark of the achievement of the guns and the crews that Russian orders forbade their tank commanders from entering into anti-tank duels with the Geschutze head to head, ordering them instead to manoeuvre to find the weaker side and rear armour.

Tank crews relax in the shelter of a Panzer III during a brief lull in the fighting during the summer of 1941.

One famous variant of the Stug IV was a real heavyweight, the forerunner of the Sturm Tiger. This was the mighty Brumbar (the grizzly bear, or grumbler), which carried a powerful 15cm Howitzer. The Brumbar had sloping frontal armour 100mm thick and was designed to rumble up to infantry fortifications before firing its massive shell at point blank range.

The Brumbar was originally developed to cope with the close-quarter street fighting at Stalingrad but delays in production meant that they did not see active service until the battle of Kursk in 1943.

After Kursk, Germany was largely fighting a defensive war, but on the few occasions when the Brumbar saw action they acquitted themselves well, and over three hundred were produced by the end of the war.

The eventual production of Sturmgeschütze totalled some 11,500 vehicles, more than any other mark of German fighting vehicle. There were sound reasons for this, as not only was the Sturmgeschütz successful on the battlefield, it was also far less expensive, quicker and easier to manufacture than fully turreted tanks built on the same chassis - a vital consideration for Germany's hard pressed manufacturing industry. German armies on all fronts were desperate for armoured fighting vehicles to stem the flood of Russian and allied armour, so production resources were increasingly switched to the production of Sturmgeschütze, which were well suited to fighting a defensive war.

THE FINAL ACT IN THE DESERT

"A tank battle of extreme violence developed with heavy casualties on both sides. Their ammunition supply was inexhaustible. Our situation on the other hand was now desperate. During the course of the day we shot off 450 tonnes of ammunition and received only 190 tonnes. Even that was delivered by destroyers to Tobruk, 300 miles away"

LIEUTENANT-GENERAL FRITZ BAYERLEIN, ON EL ALAMEIN

In the weeks that followed the battle of Alam el Halfa a steady supply of reinforcements, munitions and supplies poured into the British camp. The Sherman M3 Medium tank known to the British as 'The Grant' greatly strengthened British firepower with its 75mm gun. Montgomery was preparing to attack the German's position at El Alamein but had resolved that the men under his command would never be needlessly sacrificed. The offensive would begin on the night of 23rd October 1942.

As the initial 1000 gun artillery barrage began, the British and Commonwealth forces outnumbered the Germans and Italians almost two-to-one in men and tanks, and had vastly superior air power. Montgomery could rapidly make good any losses, with the Royal Navy dominating the Mediterranean; Rommel could not. More critically, the Afrika Korps possessed only one-tenth of the fuel which they required for full operational mobility, and operations would soon be restricted. There had also been widespread outbreaks of disease amongst the German forces and Rommel himself had fallen ill. On the first day of the battle of El Alamein Rommel was convalescing in Austria.

Montgomery's initial plan was for a major thrust to the north screened by a feint to the south. The first two days were spent probing passages through the deep minefields in what Montgomery called the 'crumbling process' - the wearing down of the enemy's entrenched defences. The

A Tiger on its way to the front is the subject of intense interest from the locals during the final battles for Tunisia.

German anti-tank positions proved too resilient and the hope for breakthrough into the open desert to the German rear did not succeed.

The adaptable Montgomery decided on a change of tactics and on 28th October he struck north towards the coast. Rommel rapidly and successfully countered. In these fierce tank battles the Germans were destroying four machines for every one lost. Montgomery again changed tactics and a third attack began on November 2nd. It met with fierce resistance and at the end of the day 200 tanks on both sides were out of action, but a corridor had been forced through the German defences. The two armoured divisions comprising the main striking arm of the Afrika Korps had now dwindled to 2,000 men and some thirty-five tanks.

On 3rd November Rommel was forced to organise a general withdrawal. Montgomery had won the battle for El Alamein.

It was now that Montgomery's instinctive caution worked against him. The follow-up was slow and hesitant. With a combination of skill and luck Rommel's small forces eluded the vastly superior British and Commonwealth forces. However, Operation Torch was just round the corner and on 8th November British and American Forces began to land in north-west Africa. Rommel launched his last counter-attack on 16th March in an attempt to hold the Mareth line in Libya, but it was easily beaten off. Shortly thereafter he was recalled to Germany. Hitler was disappointed in his Field Marshall but he wanted him well out of the way before the ignominy of final capitulation.

TIGERS IN THE DESERT

The Western Allies first encountered the legendary Tiger tank in Tunisia in December 1942. Rommel's desert war had been going from bad to worse for the hard pressed men of the Afrika Korps, and they urgently needed a morale booster. They got it in the form of the new Panzer VI – the Tiger. Its appearance came as an unpleasant surprise and was a shock to the Allies. The Tiger boasted a squat purposeful shape, and its deadly high velocity gun attained such notoriety that soon the mere appearance of the Tiger on the battlefield was enough to cause panic in the allied forces. The psychological power of the Tiger legend was so powerful that the sighting of any German tank force was enough to set the rumour running that Tigers were on the way.

With the very limited numbers which actually reached Tunisia, the Tiger menace was in some respects as much psychological as physical; nonetheless, that was no consolation for the allied tank crews who actually met the Tiger. Tank crews of the Allied Forces were disadvantaged by the superior range, killing power and armour of the Tigers. Allied tank men watched in horror as their own shells simply bounced off its thick armour plate.

In response to the Allied landings under Operation Torch in November 1942, the German high command had at last sent reinforcements to the hard pressed German forces in Tunisia. At an earlier meeting, Hitler had personally promised Rommel that he would have the new Tiger tank as soon as it was available and, sure enough, it was among the reinforcements to arrive in Tunisia, but as with all of Hitler's pledges, there were certain omissions.

The actual Tiger strength which appeared was just two companies of Schwere Panzer Abteilung 501, with 18 tigers each, and one company of the Schwere Panzer Abteilung 504 with eight machines. These units later merged to form one Abteilung.

The miracle machines were in such short supply that it led to a certain amount of unseemly squabbling among the German commanders. Field Marshall Rommel recorded that, before the start of his thrust towards Tebessa, he had asked General Von Arnim to send him the 19 Tiger tanks that were with the Fifth Panzer Army. Von Arnim demurred on the grounds that all Tigers were undergoing repair. Rommel later pointed out with some pique that this statement was patently untrue.

Against all expectations a British Army unit, 48 Royal Tank Regiment, actually captured one of the precious Tigers at Medjez El Bab on 21st April 1943. The Tigers, in company with supporting Panzer III and IV tanks, had already taken out the leading machines in a formation of Churchill tanks, when a shot from one of the remaining Churchill's six-pounder guns hit the bottom of the Tigers' gun mantlet The shell was deflected into the turret ring, which jammed the gun turret. Another shell then hit a turret lifting bracket and wounded the Tiger's commander. The German crew then abandoned the Tiger, allowing the British to capture an intact tank.

Shipped back to Britain, the tank was stripped down and provided much intelligence on German tank technology. That same Tiger tank, number 131 of 504 Schwere Panzer Abteilung, now rests at Bovington Tank museum. England.

Having been forced out of Libya and with German forces now in and around Mareth, Rommel intended to concentrate the mass of his motorised force and attack the British/American Forces in Western Tunisia with the aim of forcing withdrawal. This operation, code named 'Spring Wind', saw the capture of the Paid and Kasserine Passes through the hills as crucial. Rommel stated that he feared no effective attack from Montgomery during this phase, until the British had mustered powerful air and artillery forces.

The 21st Panzer Division, up to strength again and now under the command of 5th Panzer Army Afrika, was to attack Paid pass. The pass was required as a start point for the thrust to Sidi Banzed and Sbeitla. The attack was a success, resulting in the capture of over one thousand six hundred American prisoners and 150 tanks, including 86 US medium tanks. All of these machines were part of the US First Division.

With the movement of the Germans in the area the Allies put all forces they could muster into northern Tunisia. Fighting came down to control of the passes. The weather made the going bad for vehicles but at the same time kept the Allied Air Force at home. Air attacks would have been disastrous within the confines of the narrow passes.

Rommel thought the Allies weaker at Kasserine than at Sbiba, therefore he placed the weight of his attack there on 20th February 1943. Panzer Grenadier Regiment 'Menton' attacked, but was halted by well-placed American artillery and mortar fire from the surrounding hills. The 10th Panzer Division's Motor Cycle Battalion was thrown in to the fray. 'Nebelwerfers' were also deployed for the first time in Africa and proved very effective. By 5pm the Germans controlled the Kasserine Pass.

A US Armoured Group situated in a side pass was to have aided the Kasserine defenders. Rommel pushed the 8th Panzer Regiment across the Hatab River and caught this US Force by surprise.

Opening fire at point-blank range the Germans devastated the Americans. The 8th Panzer

A constant flow of Ju-52 transport aircraft was required to ferry in fuel, are seen being collected together in the foreground.

A Panzer IV rolls past the wreckage of a knocked-out British light tank in the Western desert campaign in 1943.

Division also captured 20 US tanks and 30 armoured troop carriers, most of which were towing 75mm anti-tank guns.

Rommel kept the 10th Panzer Division and the Afrika Korps column around the Kasserine area in case of a counter attack. However, during the night they moved northwards along the Kasserine-Thalu road and westwards to Tebessa. But the enemy had gone.

Driving through the debris of the aftermath of the battles Rommel was impressed with the Americans who the Germans had described as 'fantastically well equipped'. He went on to say: 'We (the Germans) had a lot to learn organisationally. One particularly striking feature was the standardisation of their vehicles and spare parts'. British experience had been put to good use in American equipment.

Although the Tigers had played a major part in the battle it would be true to say that, had the allied planes put in an appearance, things would have been very different. Also, of course, for the American troops it was their first meeting with the Panzers.

UPGRADING THE GERMAN ARMOUR

During 1942 the German response to the superior numbers of allied tanks lay in the development of more new tanks and up-gunning existing models. The Tiger and Panther were on their way, but in the meantime the Panzer IV was now the mainstay of the German Tank Divisions and it was still found to be capable of further development.

Only a few modifications were required to upgrade the tank to accept the highly effective long-barrelled L/43 gun, although the gun itself had to be fitted with a muzzle brake in order to prevent the gun recoil from taking off the breechblock. (The muzzle brake on a gun is fitted on the barrelled end to allow gases to vent from behind the shell before it leaves the muzzle, thus reducing the recoil force). Many of the early Panzer IVs were actually fitted with the new long L/43 gun in the field.

The last variants of the Panzer IV to appear in Africa were fitted with a more powerful gun, the L/48, which fired a shell at even higher velocity.

The Panzer IIIs in the desert theatre were also modified. The increased use of the Panzer IV in the anti-tank role left a need for infantry support tanks. The British called these upgraded tanks the 'Specials'. As the Panzer IV was being fitted with the long-barrelled 75mm the Panzer III was now fitted with the short-barrelled infantry support gun which had originally equipped the Panzer IV. In effect the two tanks had swapped roles in mid-campaign.

After the fall of Tripoli on 23rd January 1943 the Afrika Korps fell back before the advancing

British Eighth Army. The Germans left in their wake mines, booby traps and demolitions. These caused problems for the British troops unable to deploy off the main axis route due to salt marshes and soft sand.

The Germans next stand was at the Tadjera hills, which sat on the approach to the Mareth Line. A brilliant move by 22nd Army Tank Brigade put the British in a position to bring effective fire upon the Germans. This resulted in the German forces abandoning the Tadjera position, allowing British observation of the Mareth Line.

The Mareth Line lay 80 miles inside the frontier of Tunisia between the sea and the Matmata hills. The Mareth Line has been over-rated as a defensive line. The original defences were a line of antiquated blockhouses built by the French, of little use in modern warfare, except as shelter from artillery fire. The French had also believed that either a salt marsh or steep wadis would stop attackers, and that it could not be outflanked.

Rommel's inspection of the area led him to believe that well-trained soldiers could surmount these difficulties. The British advance proved him correct.

Rommel had wished to concentrate on the Akarit line, which could not be outflanked, but his superiors thought otherwise. On 15th February 1943 the rearguard of the 15th Panzer Division took up these positions in the Mareth Line. The long retreat from El Alamein was over.

This was Rommel's command position from which he commanded his last action in the desert war; the writing was on the wall for the Afrika Korps.

Rommel, now a disillusioned and physically sick man, was ordered to leave his beloved Africa Korps on 9th March 1943. He flew back to Europe, deep in despair about the approach of the inevitable end. Hitler this time refused to allow him to return to Africa where his men, now under the command of General von Armin, soldiered on. The axis forces retreated all the way into Tunisia and to Enfidaville, some twenty-five miles south of the Cape Bon peninsula and between the mountains and the sea. Here the 90th Light Division dug in around the hills while the 21st Panzer Division prepared to meet a head on thrust from the massed allied forces.

During the first days of May an incredibly ferocious artillery and air bombardment ripped into the German positions. At the heart of the defence of Tunis the 15th Panzer made a desperate last attempt to combat the overwhelming allied forces.

The guns fired until there was no more ammunition. The tanks, when their petrol was gone, carried on firing from where they stopped until they, too, ran out of ammunition. The official

Inspecting one of a group of knocked-out British Matildas. These machines were taken and used by the Afrika Korps in surprisingly large numbers.

A Bersaglieri despatch rider from the Italian Ariete division arriving with a message at an Sd. Kfz. 263 eight-wheeled radio car.

report of Army Group Africa preserved to this day, records simply: 'The bulk of 15th Panzer Division must be deemed to have been destroyed'.

In early May, slowly, reluctantly, the white flags of surrender began to appear from the men whom Hitler had ordered to fight to the last. The allies marched triumphantly into Tunis. Rommel's Afrika Korps had existed for two years and three months. Out-gunned, out-supplied, out-numbered, but rarely out-manoeuvred, the Afrika Korps marched proudly into the pages of German military

CAPTURED ALLIED TANKS

The four-man American M4 Sherman medium tank armed with the 75mm gun was to become the main and most numerous American produced tank of the war. The DAK first encountered British-operated Shermans in October 1942, and then American operated Shermans in Tunisia. A small number of Shermans were captured by the Afrika Korps and designated as Panzerkampfwagen M4 748(a). One particular machine nicknamed 'War Daddy' from the 3rd Battalion of the 5th American Armoured Division, captured by Corporal Thull of the 501st Schwere Panzer Abteilung, a heavy tank unit equipped with Tiger tanks. It was taken on 22nd February 1943, near Sbeitla in Tunisia, and shortly after was sent over to the Army Weapons Office in Germany for evaluation and tests. Later on, in mid-1943, 'War Daddy' took part in the tests with early model Panther Ausf D to 'prove' the Panther's superiority, which were staged for propaganda purposes. In the resulting newsreel the enthusiastic commentator shrieked with delight as the American-made machine failed to live up to the performance of the Panther. 'General Sherman fell back. His German opponent, our new heavy tank, succeeds where the Yankee failed'. Although the entire comparison was made to boost the German morale, it is well worth searching out a copy of the film for the tank enthusiast.

PANZERKAMPFWAGEN VI SD.KFZ. 182

Nicknamed the 'furniture van' by the Germans because of its bulkiness and 57 ton weight, the Panzer VI went into production in 1942 following further demands from Hitler that the Army needed heavier tanks. Henschel and Porsche both submitted prototypes, but Henschel was chosen as the manufacturer as his design appeared to break down less than Porsche's design. The 'Tiger Model E', as it was first called, initially saw military action at Leningrad in August 1942.

The Model E, designated Tiger I, equipped the special heavy tank units of the Wehrmacht and the Waffen-SS and saw service until the end of the war. However, like the Panther, the Tiger entered service too early and was faced with technical difficulties resulting in continual breakdowns. The Tiger I had the powerful 88mm gun and thick frontal armour making it virtually indestructible. In late 1942 British troops in Tunisia met the Tiger I and soon discovered that two of the main problems with the Tiger were its thin rear armour plate and an engine which demanded constant maintenance.

Two types of Tiger I were produced - the Ausf H and the Ausf E (HI) – both were soon replaced by the introduction of the Tiger II, designed in 1943.

From July 1942, only 1,355 were manufactured by Henschel and Wegmann with production continuing as late as August of 1944. Tiger production reached its highest point in April 1944, when 105 were produced. The main reasons for the low numbers were the Tiger's difficult production and its cost. Out of the entire number produced some 500 saw service with SS heavy tank units. A very small number of Tigers were sold to Hungary in 1944. On June 7th 1943 the Japanese ambassador in Germany, General Oshima, was shown a Tiger from sPzAbt 502. A single Tiger was then sold to Japan in 1943, but was never delivered due to the war situation and was loaned by Japan to the German Army (sSSPzAbt 101). Henschel charged Japan 645.000 Reichsmarks for the fully equipped Tiger (with ammunition and radio equipment), while the regular price for the same Tiger was only 300.000 ReichsMarks. Some sources state that Spain was interested in acquiring a number of Tigers but the transaction was never finalized.

The Department of Weaponry of the Red Army made these interesting observations in late 1944:

"It is suggested to the Red Army to use such German tanks as StuG III and Pz IV due to their reliability and availability of spare parts. The new German Panther and Tiger can be used until they are broken down without trying to repair them. They have bad engines, transmission and suspension."

A Tiger I assigned to the SS-Pz. Korps "Leibstandarte Adolf Hitler" operating in France.

Tigers were equipped with two kinds of tracks. 520mm narrow tracks (used for transportation) and 720mm battle (wider) tracks. Also special railroad flatbed cars were produced in order to transport and unload Tigers more quickly. From mid-1943, Tigers were very commonly coated with Zimmerite anti-magnetic paste. Late production Tigers differed slightly from early models and shared many common parts with the Panzer V Panther in order to simplify their production. There was also an experimental mounting of the 88mm KwK 43 L/71 gun on the Tiger E but it was delayed and abandoned in favour of the development of Tiger II, which eventually replaced the Tiger I. The massive Panzerkampfwagen VI Tiger will remain forever a symbol of formidable German Panzer formations of World War II.

Armour (mm/angle) Ausf A.
Front Turret: 100/8
Front Upper Hull: 100/10
Front Lower Hull: 100/24
Side Turret: 80/0
Side Upper Hull: 80/0
Side Lower Hull: 80/8
Rear Turret: 80/0
Rear Hull: 80/8
Turret Top/ Bottom: 25/81-90
Upper Hull Top / Bottom: 25/90
Lower Hull Top / Bottom: 25/90
Gun Mantlet: 100-110/0

Model	Ausf H/E
Weight	56.9 tonnes
Crew	5
Engine	Ausf H - Maybach HL210 P 45, V-12, 650 bhp Ausf E - Maybach HL230 P 45, V-12, 700 bhp
Speed (Road)	38 km/h
Range	Road: 90 km Crosscountry: 60 km
Fuel Capacity	534 litres
Length	8.24 m
Width	3.73 m
Height	2.88 m
Armament	L/56 & 2 x 7.92mm MG

The crew of a Tiger make essential checks before moving into action during the winter of 1942/1943.

CONVERSIONS

- **Befehlswagen Tiger I Ausf. E (Sd. Kfz 267/268)** - command tank
- **Sturmpanzer (Sturmmorser) Sturmtiger Ausf E** - heavy mortar carrier
- **Bergewagen Bergetiger** - heavy recovery vehicle
- **Tiger (P)** - Porsche design (5 produced)
- **Schwerst-Flammpanzer auf Tiger I** - long range flamethrower tank (planned)
- **Sturmpanzer Bar** - 305mm L/16 gun carrier (planned)
- **Sturmpanzer Tiger I** - 170mm Kanone 44 gun carrier
- **Sturmpanzer Tiger I** - 210mm Moerser 18/43 mortar carrier (project)
- **Sturmpanzer Tiger I** - Skoda's 305mm Granatwefer heavy mortar carrier (project)
- **Tiger I** - 240mm Kanone 4 transport vehicle (project)
- **Panzerkampfwagen VI Tiger II Ausf B**

More from the same series

Most books from the 'Hitler's War Machine' series are edited and endorsed by Emmy Award winning film maker and military historian Bob Carruthers, producer of Discovery Channel's Line of Fire and Weapons of War and BBC's Both Sides of the Line. Long experience and strong editorial control gives the military history enthusiast the ability to buy with confidence.

Tiger I in Combat

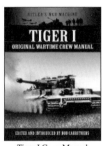
Tiger I Crew Manual

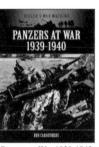
Panzers at War 1939-1942

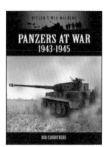
Panzers at War 1943-1945

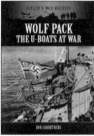
Wolf Pack - the U boats

Poland 1939

Luftwaffe Combat Reports

Sturmgeschütze

German Artillery in Combat

Panzer Combat Reports

The Panther V in Combat

German Tank Hunters

The Afrika Korps in Combat

Panzers I & II

Panzer III

Panzer IV

For more information visit www.pen-and-sword.co.uk